BIG IDEAS

For a Better Sunday School

With

Special Sundays for Every Sunday of the Year

By

Rev. Clarence Sexton

Pastor Temple Baptist Church
Beaver Creek Drive
At Adams Creek Drive
Powell, TN 37849

SWORD of the LORD
PUBLISHERS
P.O.BOX 1099, MURFREESBORO, TN 37133

ACKNOWLEDGMENT

I want to express my gratitude to Bernard D. Dodrill. Without his efforts, this book could never have been in print.

The Author

Printed in U.S.A.

ISBN 0—87398—080—8

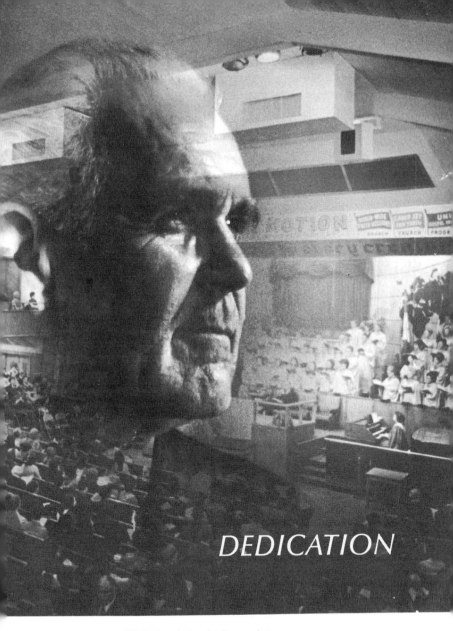

DEDICATION

This book is dedicated to

D R .   L E E   R O B E R S O N

He is the most Christ-like person I know. I am honored by his friendship and constantly inspired by his example.

Preface

Inspiration and ideas are two things that all of us as Christian workers need most in our ministry. Inspiration to give our best to God in dedicated service should come as we view the sin-sick, Christ-rejecting world around us.

Ideas to help us reach the world for Christ come from many sources, one of which is a book that Rev. Clarence Sexton has compiled.

Having been totally involved in the ministry of the Highland Park Baptist Church for nearly thirty years, I have seen most of these ideas developed and used effectively.

I commend Brother Sexton for the excellent work he has done in making this material available in this form to pastors and Sunday School workers.

It is the prayer of all of us connected with the Highland Park Baptist Church that God will bless the ministry of these pages to the salvation of many precious souls.

Dr. J. R. Faulkner
Highland Park Baptist Church

Table of Contents

Introduction

The ideas found in this book are ideas that have proven successful at the Highland Park Baptist Church in Chattanooga, Tennessee. Every Sunday is a special day at Highland Park. The Word of God is faithfully proclaimed, souls are saved, converts are baptized, and Christians are challenged to greater service. Our Sunday School is presently averaging over 9,400 Sunday after Sunday. Last year over 3,400 people made professions of faith and followed the Lord in baptism. The blessing of God upon all the work is phenomenal. Every ministry continues to grow year after year — "always more than the year before" — especially the Sunday School.

The primary reason for this is, of course, the blessing of God upon a man — Dr. Lee Roberson, our pastor. He is a man of vision, compassion, and great wisdom. There are not words adequate to describe the admiration and respect held by the membership of the Highland Park Baptist Church for Dr. Roberson and his associate, Dr. J. R. Faulkner. Suffice it to say that these are "holy men of God."

Dr. Roberson has encouraged the highest quality of teaching and living on the part of those who serve in positions of leadership in the Sunday School and has, at the same time, made excellent use of the basic principles of Sunday School growth to build one of the world's great Sunday Schools. These principles and ideas are given to you in this book — put them to use! My prayer is that every idea may prove to be of value and help to you in reaching the lost and building a great Sunday School.

Clarence Sexton, 1978

Highland Park Baptist Church. Old wooden tabernacle used from 1943 to 1947.

1

Determine to Have A Great Sunday School

"Many dream but few pay the price to make a dream become a reality."

There is a certain danger in stating standards of greatness. Yet, one must admit there are particular things that ought to be a part of every Sunday School that desires to be great for God's eternal glory. These are the things found in every great Sunday School. If these are true of every Sunday School, they should be evident in every Sunday School class and in the life of every Sunday School worker.

REACHES ALL PEOPLE

Now some Sunday Schools in America are big, but they are not great because they shun a certain group of people. They shun them because of race, social standing, the area where they live, or perhaps because of the discipline problems they encounter in working with them. For some reason, they decide not to reach a certain group. That Sunday School, no matter how large, is not great. "For God so loved the *world* that He gave His only begotten Son, that whosoever believeth in Him should not perish, but have everlasting life." John 3:16

TEACHES THE WORD OF GOD

The greatest asset to any Sunday School is not promotions but the uninterrupted teaching and preaching of the Word of God. Promotion is good to bait the hook to get fish on the line in order to pull them in. Promotion and big days and big ideas are excellent, but promotions only get them to come. A program of uninterrupted Bible teaching will keep them.

HAS A TEACHERS' MEETING

Look at the business world. Any business that is succeeding has a time when the personnel comes together and meets to discuss problems and better methods of business. The leadership of a Sunday School also needs a time to meet. A great Sunday School has a teachers' meeting.

IS A SOUL-WINNING ORGANIZATION

The cutting edge of the church is the Sunday School because the Sunday School is the one organization that is given, more than anything else, to soul winning.

WORKS ON ENROLLMENT

We are talking about getting people on the Sunday School roll. Make them our responsibility. Every person that rides a bus or attends should be on the Sunday School roll. We have to get the names of every boy or girl that comes into our class or we are not going to be what God wants us to be. Enroll anyone, anywhere, anytime if that person is not already on a Sunday School roll and is willing to be enrolled in your class. Never drop anyone from the roll unless that person has died, moved to another city, or has joined another church.

HAS HIGH STANDARDS FOR TEACHERS AND WORKERS

They must know they are saved, live separated from the world, be faithful to the church, and loyal to the leadership.

HAS A WEEKLY VISITATION PROGRAM

We cannot be what we ought to be in the Sunday School if we are not visiting. It does not matter who we are or what we do; we have got to go after people. We cannot understand them, we will not love them, we cannot win them, if we do not go after them.

HAS DEFINITE GOALS

If you shoot at nothing, you hit nothing. A great Sunday School has goals. That means for leaders, teachers, classes — goals.

A GREAT SUNDAY SCHOOL GROWS

People say, "Oh, your church is too big for me." Why do people come here? Because the blessing of God is upon it. It is growing because God is blessing it. Do not ever apologize. If a Sunday School is not growing, it is not functioning as God wants it to function.

CHECKLIST

	YES	NO
Are you reaching all people?	———	———
Are you teaching the Word of God?	———	———
Do you have a weekly teacher's meeting?	———	———
Are you winning souls?	———	———
Are you enlisting new members?	———	———
Do you have high standards for teachers and workers?	———	———
Do you have a weekly visitation program?	———	———
Do you have definite goals?	———	———
Is your Sunday School growing?	———	———

2

Look at the Example Given Through History

> *"Every great movement can be traced to a kneeling figure."*
>
> D. L. Moody

The work of the Sunday School is the work of reaching people. From the birth of the modern-day Sunday School movement in the town of Gloucester, England, over 150 years ago until this present time, the Sunday School has been a means used by Bible believers to, first, evangelize the lost, and then educate the saved.

Of course, it has always been God's plan to have His Word taught. The Lord gave parents the responsibility of teaching their children.

> *For he established a testimony in Jacob, and appointed a law in Israel, which he commanded our fathers, that they should make them known to their children: That the generation to come might know them, even the children which should be born; who should arise and declare them to their children.*
>
> *Psalm 78:5-6*

> *And these words, which I command thee this day, shall be in thine heart: And thou shalt teach them diligently unto thy children, and shalt talk of them when thou sittest in thine house, and when thou walkest by the way, and when thou liest down, and when thou risest up.*
>
> *Deuteronomy 6:6-7*

> *Therefore shall ye lay up these my words in your heart and in your soul, and bind them for a sign upon your hand, that they may be as frontlets between your eyes. And ye shall teach them your children, speaking of them when thou sittest in thine house, and when thou walkest by the way,*

> *when thou liest down, and when thou risest up. And thou*
> *shalt write them upon the doorposts of thine house, and*
> *upon thy gates.*   *Deuteronomy 11:18-20*

Parents were instructed by the Lord to patiently and earnestly teach their children the Word of God.

We also notice that the job of the priest was to publicly teach and give instruction in God's Word.

> *And Moses wrote this law, and delivered it unto the*
> *priests the sons of Levi, which bare the ark of the covenant of*
> *the LORD, and unto all the elders of Israel. And Moses*
> *commanded them, saying, At the end of every seven years, in*
> *the solemnity of the year of release, in the feast of taberna-*
> *cles, When all Israel is come to appear before the LORD thy*
> *God in the place which he shall choose, thou shalt read this*
> *law before all Israel in their hearing. Gather the people*
> *together, men, and women, and children, and thy stranger*
> *that is within thy gates, that they may hear, and that they*
> *may learn, and fear the LORD your God, and observe to do*
> *all the words of this law: And that their children, which*
> *have not known any thing, may hear, and learn to fear the*
> *LORD your God, as long as ye live in the land whither ye go*
> *over Jordan to possess it.*   *Deuteronomy 31:9-13*

God made the teaching of His Word such an important matter that He set aside the entire tribe of Levi to educate all the other people. All their time was to be given over to this task. They were supported from the tithes of the people.

As a result of the failure of the priesthood to teach the Word of God, we find the rise of the school of prophets. Samuel, the first of the prophets, started a system of Bible instruction, after which our Bible institutes of today are patterned. The first school of the prophets was at Ramah (I Samuel 19:19-20). Others sprang up in Bethel, Jericho, Gilgal, and elsewhere. (Notice early chapters of II Kings.)

Just prior to the time of Christ, we find the wide use of synagogues in teaching the Word of God. In these synagogues the rabbi taught the people. All ages of the Jewish population could be found in these synagogues being taught God's Word. Some historians have noted that there were at one time nearly five hundred synagogues in the city of Jerusalem alone where the Word of God was being taught.

As one reads the New Testament, he immediately sees that the Lord Jesus was recognized by those who knew Him as a teacher. Time after time in the gospel record He was addressed as a teacher. When Nicodemus came to Him under the cover of darkness, he addressed Him as Rabbi, or Teacher. The disciples also taught the Word of God. The great missionary, Paul, was a Bible teacher. He planted new churches, taught them God's Word, and instructed them to teach others.

When Robert Raikes decided in Gloucester, England, in the year 1780, to teach the Bible to a regiment of ragged boys, he was only reviving biblical principles that had already been established.

Robert Raikes, born in 1736, was a successful newspaper editor by the age of 22. He expressed a great desire to help humanity and often made public his opinions in his paper, the *Gloucester Journal*. His first attempts were to rehabilitate prisoners, but his efforts were somewhat fruitless. Reports came to Raikes one day of a band of rowdy boys that were causing quite a disturbance in a certain section of town. He was asked to condemn the acts of these boys in his paper, but instead he chose to go down to the troubled spot and see firsthand what was happening. Mr. Raikes was already very troubled over the abuse of children serving as laborers working long hours on difficult jobs. Education of children in his day was a luxury afforded only by the wealthy, but Robert Raikes felt that these ragged boys deserved an opportunity to learn. He hired four teachers to teach these boys the Bible. The kitchen of a Christian woman named Mrs. Meredith was used for a classroom. Mr. Raikes worked very hard to get the boys to attend the classes, which were conducted on Sundays. They began at 10:00 a.m., took a break at noon, and resumed after lunch. The children were taught to read and were given lessons from the Bible.

Most churches were very hostile to Mr. Raikes' Sunday School movement in the beginning; but he soon found a friend in John Wesley, the famous founder of Methodism. John Wesley gave his approval to the Sunday School movement and earnestly urged every Methodist Society to start a Sunday School. By the time of Robert Raikes' death in 1811, there were over 400,000 people enrolled in Sunday Schools in England.

Although this movement began in England, it rose to its

greatest heights in America. The first record of a Sunday School in America was the one conducted by William Elliot in Oak Grove, Virginia, in 1785. Francis Asbury, the great Methodist preacher and evangelist, was also involved with the Sunday School movement during its earliest days in America.

One of the most famous stories related by Sunday School historians is about a man named Stephen Paxson. Paxson's daughter was challenged by her Sunday School teacher to bring a new pupil. Mr. Paxson was a handicapped man, having a stutter and a limp. He loved music and played fiddle for the Saturday night square dance. After the urging of his daughter, he attended the Sunday School class. Upon hearing the Gospel, he gave his heart to Christ and soon surrendered his life to serve the Lord in the pioneer work of starting Sunday Schools. Mr. Paxson is said to have traveled over 100,000 miles on horseback, started 1,314 Sunday Schools, and seen 83,000 children saved. God give us more Stephen Paxsons.

As the Sunday School movement has progressed through the years and comes to this present point in history, it brings to us the greatest opportunity on the face of the earth to evangelize the unsaved.

3

Get Your Purpose Straight

"It is not how long people live, but how much they live that matters most. Life is not measured or evaluated by birth-dates but by deeds."

Dr. R. G. Lee

People passing through the park of a certain city would stop and gaze at a man with a hammer and chisel in his hand, working on a beautiful piece of stone. Of course, everyone wondered what the sculptor was designing. Finally, one passerby could stand it no longer. He approached the man and asked, "Sir, what are you forming from this beautiful stone?" The man replied, "Oh, I am not making anything. I am just chiseling."

This is the problem with most of us in the work of the Lord. We are just chiseling. Let us determine to get the purpose of our Sunday School straight and work at it with all our might.

It is most difficult to attempt anything without a definite purpose in mind, and it is impossible to build a great Sunday School without a purpose. What is the purpose of the Sunday School?

WIN THE UNSAVED

The Sunday School must be a soul-winning organization. Our task is to carry out the Great Commission. We must be faithful to win the lost.

BAPTIZE THE SAVED

The first step of obedience as a Christian is to follow Christ in the ordinance of baptism. Many are on our rolls in Sunday School who have never been baptized since they were saved. The job of the Sunday School is to instruct them in this step of obedience.

TEACH THE WORD OF GOD

Much is said about the Word of God, but too little of the Bible is being actually taught pupils in Sunday School. We must give folks the Bible on the level which they understand.

PROMOTE FAITHFULNESS

The best thing that can be said about a Christian is that that person is faithful — faithful to Christ, to God's Word, and faithful to the church. The best organization in the church to stress the importance of being in God's house Sunday morning, Sunday night, and Wednesday night is the Sunday School.

ENCOURAGE WORSHIP

A tremendous mistake is made by those who come to Sunday School and do not stay for the worship service. Great harm is done also by those who bring children to Sunday School and take them home before the worship service. Man must have a time to worship God, and the Sunday School should stress the importance of this.

TEACH GOOD STEWARDSHIP

A selfish spirit prevails in so much of the world today. Men know nothing of their responsibility before God as stewards. The Sunday School must set itself to the task of teaching the "grace of giving."

REACH ALL THE FAMILY

It is wrong to think of the Sunday School as an organization only for children. It is also wrong for a church to choose to place all its emphasis on reaching only a certain age with the Word of God. The one organization of the local church that has the greatest opportunity to reach all the family is the Sunday School. God help us to go through this open door.

4

America Needs Your Sunday School

"Is there not a cause?"
I Samuel 17:29

I shall never forget a heart-stirring story that was related to me shortly after I answered the call to preach. It went like this. A certain businessman in a northern city left for his office one morning only to find when arriving that his company had gone bankrupt and his fortune had crumbled. He left the office and drove back toward home. Depressed and with all desire to live gone, he stopped at a pawn shop on the way home and purchased a pistol. When he drove up in front of his house, he loaded the gun and walked toward his front door. Upon entering his home, he called his family into the living room. He pulled the gun from his pocket, shot every member of his family, put the gun to his own head, and pulled the trigger. He thought he had killed everyone, but his little daughter, severely wounded but very much alive, staggered to the telephone and began to dial. She had memorized a number she was to call in case of an emergency. When the neighbor picked up the phone, the little girl said, "Daddy shot me, everybody is dead, and I am all alone."

I believe this is the picture of our country. America needs your Sunday School.

Many Sunday Schools in America fall into a rut, and the leadership fails to realize the value of the work being done. There is nothing in the world more important than the teaching of the Word of God. The following reasons are given for this conviction.

The Sunday School Is the Only Place of Bible Teaching for Most People

Think about the activities of boys and girls, men and women; and you find no other place during the week where they hear the Word of God taught. The vital importance of the Sunday School is seen when one realizes it is the only place of Bible instruction for most.

Moms and Dads Are Not Teaching
Their Children the Word of God

The ideal home situation is to have a Christian parent sit down and teach his children the Word of God. The truth is, this is not being done. The American home is on the rocks and not on the Rock, Christ Jesus. Most parents are unsaved. Many homes are broken, and there is certainly not a Bible-teaching program going on.

The Public Schools for the Most Part Are Anti-Bible

One man who recently gave his heart to Christ and was gloriously saved stated that in the country where he was from it was felt that one was not scholarly if he believed the Bible — he was from Communist Russia! Sad, but how true it is — multitudes in America have the same idea. The public school has declared it does not need the Bible, while the products of the public school system say by their actions they do need it. The educational philosophy today is against God. They state that man is basically good and can be educated into being anything he wishes to be. Oh, how wrong! What a responsibility all this places on the Sunday School.

The Sunday School Is Needed to Combat
Worldly Influences Upon the Lives of American People

If one simply drives the streets of America and views the masses of wasted life, he soon sees the need to get people under the sound of the Word of God. Our Sunday Schools must feel the responsibility to lift up the Word of God as a standard for life. The teaching must be interesting and exciting. People need the Bible.

The Sunday School of Today Is the Church of Tomorrow

Walk through the hallways of the children's and youth departments of the Sunday School, and you are looking at more than a part of the Sunday School of today. You are actually seeing the church leaders of tomorrow. They must be filled with the wonderful Word of God.

The Bible Is the Only Textbook for Success in Life

The words *failure* and *waste* are two words that characterize a large part of our society today. Everyone desires success, but there is no success apart from the Bible and Bible principles for living. We are to do more in our Sunday School than bring people together for one hour on Sunday morning for a period of information and instruction. We are in reality standing before precious souls with the only hope for eternal life and the only textbook for successful living. This is important. As a matter of fact, there is nothing in all the world any more important. America needs your Sunday School!

CHAPTER

5

Put Principles of Growth to Work

"Growth is the only real sign of life."

A discouraged Pastor called recently and said, "I need help. My church is not growing. My people are unhappy and I am unhappy. It seems like we have just died!"

Sunday Schools will stagnate if they do not grow. Some seek to choose between quantity and quality. No choice needs to be made; we can have both. When a Sunday School begins to grow and people begin to come in by the multitudes, buses fill up, people get out and win souls and bring them in—all of a sudden somebody says, "Wait a minute, wait a minute! We are not teaching and discipling all these people like we ought to be. Now let us slow all the evangelism down and begin to disciple them." That is a mistake. Once you lose the momentum of reaching people, you may be able to train a few; but the zeal for reaching them is lost. You do not have to choose. You can do both. Numerical growth is quantity. Spiritual growth is quality. Both are included in Matthew chapter 28, verses 19-20. "Go ye therefore, and teach all nations, baptizing them in the name of the Father, and of the Son, and of the Holy Ghost." That is quantity. "Teaching them to observe all things whatsoever I have commanded you: and, lo, I am with you alway, even unto the end of the world." That is quality. The Lord intends for us to do both. Someone is going to say sooner or later, "We have got a class full of kids; and, to tell you the truth, I do not think they are learning what they ought to be learning; and I do not want any more kids coming. I just tell you the truth, I do not want any more. I want to get down here with these and teach these and have a little pure group with these." Now, what are we going to say to that teacher? Let us reach all we can and teach all of those we reach.

DIFFICULTIES IN GROWTH

A Sunday School averaging two thousand can operate as effectively as a Sunday School averaging two hundred, if it is done right. There is no need to minimize either quantity or quality in reaching people or teaching people. It can all be done. This thing is like two rails of a train track—reaching is one, and teaching is the other. Do them both. Now let us be quick to admit that if we get a little ahead on one of them, let us get ahead on the reaching one. Get them saved and going to heaven.

Lack of room

Room can always be found. Do not ever forget that.

Criticism of just going after numbers

Someone will say, "All you are interested in is getting numbers." Well, every number is a precious soul that is going to live as long as God lives in heaven or hell. If they want to knock us for getting numbers, let them knock. Praise God! Let us get every number we can.

The laborers are few

Some say, "We do not have the workers." We read in Luke 10:2, "Pray ye therefore the Lord of the harvest, that he would send forth laborers into his harvest." We will get the laborers. If there is a need, God will raise them up. When there is a need, and we will step out by faith to reach the masses, God will raise up the workers. Never say, "I wish I had fewer." Let us work a little harder, find more people, and provide the room.

LAWS OF SUNDAY SCHOOL GROWTH

These are Flake's Laws of Sunday School Growth. Wherever these five things are applied, the Sunday School will grow. In any situation, anywhere in the world, it will grow.

Locate the prospects

There are people to be reached. Find the people. There are multitudes that are going to hell around most any church.

Enlarge the organization

This means prepare for an increase in number. Prepare for it. Some say, "We do not need this large classroom for this age group. We do not have that many coming now." True, but there are that many of that age group and more that we have located. We must prepare for them.

14

Enlist and train workers

Enlist and train workers. Do not just enlist them. Do not just train the ones you have. Enlist more and train them. We must have laborers. The biggest problem in the work of God is not finances, not buildings, not space, not equipment. The biggest problem is always, and will always be, and has always been — laborers. That is the number one thing to be conquered. That is what Jesus revealed to us when He said, "Pray ye therefore the Lord of the harvest." The harvest is great, but the laborers are few.

Provide space

Space is not one of the big problems. Now what are we going to do? We must locate space. Space can be found.

Go after people

We do not just build a building and do all these things and then say, "All right you sinners, come on in." It does not work that way. We must go after people.

6

Enlist and Train Workers

"God blesses and empowers people, not programs."

As mentioned briefly in an earlier chapter, the greatest need in the work of God today is not the need for buildings, equipment, or even finances. It is the need for laborers — those who are willing to do the work of God. The Lord Jesus said, "The laborers are few. . ." Luke 10:1-2.

HOW DO WE ENLIST LABORERS?

A growing Sunday School must be in a continual worker-enlistment program. Do not ever tell anyone you have no place for them — find a place. Anyone who is willing to work is an asset to the cause of Christ.

1. **Magnify the position of the servant.** Let your people know of the importance of those who serve in the work of Christ. We must have them.

2. **Write letters to new members.** In your follow-up with those who come into the church, let them know there is much to be done.

3. **Take a church-wide survey.** Find out how many of the adults in your church do not actually have a definite place of service. Some may not be qualified, but many will be.

4. **Have a Training Clinic.** Have a Sunday School workers' clinic, a bus workers' clinic, a soul-winning clinic. Invite everyone to attend. Sign them up to be present. Pray for God to speak to hearts.

5. **Notice those who are winning souls.** Any wise leader realizes the value of the soul winner. He will not only win the lost, but his work will stir others to do the same. Use him in the service of the Lord.

6. **Glean workers from special emphases.** Many workers may be found from among those who work in such special events as the Vacation Bible School.

Teachers' and Officers' meeting of Highland Park Baptist Church.

7. **Look for those who have been faithful at small tasks.** Perhaps the people who only address envelopes for the Sunday School class letter will someday be some of the most outstanding teachers. Give people a chance to prove themselves; and once they have done this, continue to elevate their responsibility.

TRAINING THE WORKERS

Many times we expect workers to perform their tasks with great effectiveness, but they fail. Much of this failure is due to the fact that they were not properly trained to do the task to which they were assigned.

1. **Workers need to serve as apprentices.** There is great value in learning how to do a certain job by working alongside someone who is already getting the job done. Every teacher needs an assistant to help and to train.

2. **Assign certain parts of the job to the prospective worker.** Allow the prospective worker to assist in certain responsibilities. He cannot carry the entire load to begin with, but he can have some responsibility in his "learning period."

3. **Provide helpful tools.** Do not give someone a job without the proper tools with which to work. Teach him how to study his Bible. Provide helpful tapes and books.

17

4. **Attend workshops and conferences.** Expose the new worker to an intensified period of training in the workshop and other helpful conferences.

RESPONSIBILITIES OF THE PASTOR AND OTHER KEY LEADERS TO THE WORKERS

Part of the responsibility of selecting workers and assigning them to certain tasks is the business of keeping them on the job. Many get started and do not remain. What can be done?

1. **Let them know they are appreciated.** Write letters, say kind things, recognize them in public meetings and do any number of other things to let them know they are appreciated.

2. **Avoid personality clashes.** Do not put the new worker with someone he cannot work with. The inability to work with this individual would not necessarily be because of spiritual problems but personality clashes.

3. **Attempt to avoid misfit jobs.** Some people get frustrated and quit because they were assigned something they just could not do. These people would have done an excellent job at a task to which they were suited, but may never work again.

4. **Try to prevent discouragement.** Discouragement is one of Satan's best weapons. Instill certain principles in the new worker that will prevent discouragement. We shall reap in due season if we faint not. The Lord will give us the victory. Remember also that discouragers always overstate their problems.

The *work* of the Lord can not be done without *workers*. May He help us to do a better job enlisting, training, and keeping folks at the task.

CHAPTER

7

Publicize Your Sunday School

"Follow divine direction."
Dr. Lee Roberson

I walked into the lobby of a motel in the heart of one of America's largest cities and asked for directions to the First Baptist Church of that city. I knew it was only a few blocks away and was sure I could get help. The desk clerk said, "I have heard of the church but I have no idea how to get there." We must work at making our churches and their locations familiar to people.

The secular world says, "It pays to advertise." They are right! Many of the multitudes of people in our cities and communities who do not attend any Sunday School are not aware of the location of our churches. Sad as it may sound, many do not even know they exist.

GOD WILL BLESS

A successful Sunday School has been a publicized Sunday School. People know where it is located, believe it can meet their needs, know a warm welcome awaits them, and have been personally touched by its ministry.

The Lord Jesus said, ". . .Go out into the highways and hedges, and compel them to come in, that my house may be filled." Luke 14:23. The early disciples said, ". . .we cannot but speak the things which we have seen and heard." Acts 4:20.

GETTING OUT THE GOSPEL

We are not by any means cheapening the Gospel by advertising; rather, we are proclaiming the Gospel, getting salvation's message to the hearts of the people. Persistent, "first-class" publicity that reaches to people in the home, on the job, and in the school, touching their hearts, will bring forth a harvest of souls. This is the purpose of publicity — to reach the unsaved, to help carry out the great commission.

Billboards (outdoor displays)

Billboard display companies will design and display publicity for your church. This may be too expensive for some, but it is very worthwhile.

Bumper Stickers

People will read the bumper sticker on your car. Instruct members to remove stickers when they trade cars. The name of your church could turn up at the wrong place.

Bulletin Inserts

Inserts for bulletins, emphasizing a certain ministry or special day, can be designed then used at the proper time.

Banners

Street streamers and banners can be used. It may be necessary to place the banner along the street rather than across the street. (Check the city laws.)

Newspaper Ads

Vary the ad in size and type. Use pictures.

News Items In The Newspaper

Most local papers welcome news from the church.

A Church Paper

A church paper can be printed and mailed to members and others in the city. Build a large mailing list in order to get much exposure.

Tracts

Attractive tracts with church name and address can be used.

Parades

Parades for special occasions attract a great deal of interest.

Buttons

Politicians have learned the value of buttons. They can be used to a great advantage in the church.

THE BEST FORM OF PUBLICITY

The best form of publicity is also the least expensive form of publicity. It is personal contact. The business world says that the best advertisement is a satisfied customer. The best publicity for your church is an enthusiastic, happy, soul-winning church member.

Other Forms of Publicity

Television

It is expensive but reaches the masses.

Radio

Use the radio extensively. Make use of spot announcements.

Telephone

Organize your people to call every person in your city who has a phone.

Mail

Cards and letters may be mailed using a bulk permit with only a small expense.

City-Wide Mailing

Certain agencies provide for businesses a mailing address for every resident in the area. They will also do a mailing for a church. The rate will be the same as charged for the businesses, but reaching every home makes the expense worthwhile.

Window Cards and Posters

Posters in windows still attract lots of attention when well done.

Pastoral Letter

There is something about receiving a letter from the pastor. When mailing is regularly used, change the color of the envelope and letterhead to add variety.

This is by no means an exhaustive list, neither is it intended to tell how to do a certain thing. It is given to provide ideas to Christian leaders in publicizing the work of the Lord. Whatever type of publicity is entered upon, do it first class or do not do it at all.

CHAPTER

8

Prepare the Sunday School for Evangelism

"Base everything on the value of precious souls."

The greatest evangelistic arm of the local church is the Sunday School; but at the same time, the Sunday School must prepare for evangelism. Soul winning does not just happen. Sunday Schools just do not all of a sudden begin to grow. If a great program of *reaching* people is to be initiated, the Sunday School must be a vital part of it; and it must, at the same time, develop the proper *teaching* program to work hand in hand, reaching people with the Gospel and teaching them the Word of God. Our existing Sunday School must go forth with a new spirit of adventure and excitement, enrolling new members in old classes and beginning new classes with a bold evangelistic thrust to reach the unsaved.

CONDUCTING A ONE-NIGHT SUNDAY SCHOOL CLINIC AND WORKSHOP

This clinic can begin with a banquet meal served to all our Sunday School officers and other prospective workers. The entire meeting, including the meal, would last no longer than two hours. Vital subjects would be discussed, such as:

1. **Responsibilities of Sunday School personnel**
2. **Methods of Sunday School enrollment**
3. **An outreach leader for each class and other class organizations**
4. **The value of courtesy and friendliness**
5. **The necessity of an overall plan for the placement of classes and age groups**
6. **The reason for the establishment of new classes**

22

A MASTER PLAN FOR LOCATING CLASSES
MUST BE DEVELOPED

The best use of all our buildings and facilities must be made. Some departments will expect greater growth. Some will need to be closer to the main auditorium of the church. Many things must be taken into consideration as the Sunday School prepares for evangelism.

New Classes Must Be Established

The greatest growth of the Sunday School takes place during the period of establishing new classes and enrolling new people. This fact, combined with the entire evangelistic program of the church which will be bringing in new people, will necessitate the establishment of new classes. Also, classes must be started to care for special groups of people that will be attending in larger numbers — groups such as the mentally retarded, the very poor, the elderly, and others.

9

We Must Reach the Cities With the Sunday School

> *"The greatest frontier facing the Christian today is not outer space but the inner city."*

Someone has said, "When life hands you a lemon, just add a little sugar and make lemonade out of it; drink it and go on." *The point is, do not let your problems stop your purpose.* The test of one's real desire to serve God and do a work for the Lord is not in what it takes to get him started but rather in what it takes to stop him after he starts.

We are faced with a new frontier. The pastor in a downtown church faces some unique problems not encountered by pastors in other locations; but there are also abundant opportunities of service available to the downtown work that are not available in other areas.

Some of the problems facing the downtown church are:

1. Too little parking.
2. The pull of the churches in the suburban areas where members live.
3. Scattered membership. The members of the church live in all areas of the city.
4. Travel to and from church.
5. Visitation. Distance must be dealt with.
6. Property. Buildings and space are needed to reach people.

PARKING CAN BE A PROBLEM

People may visit a church one or two Sundays and have to drive round and round searching for a place to park, but they will not continue to come unless adequate parking is provided. In the business world, many customers state that they have left the downtown shopping areas and find it so much more conve-

Parking attendants make parking a pleasure.

nient to shop in the shopping centers because they can never find a place to park downtown. Our downtown churches must provide parking. One suggestion used by a number of churches is:

"Park and Ride"

This is a unique program for providing additional parking during the worship services. This would be of great help to the church and made very enjoyable and convenient for those that participate.

1. Parking lots within a 5-8 minute distance from the church would be located. These could be business lots or factory lots that are not in use on Sundays. Permission to use these lots on Sunday morning would be gained from those in charge. (There would be many lots available—some very large.)

2. A bus would be contracted to shuttle people from this lot to the church and back.

3. The bus could make a loop covering several lots or could work strictly from one large lot.

4. The bus could be in the parking lot by 9:00 a.m.; and as soon as it was loaded, it could make the trip to the church and back, allowing after the first trip to make this trip every 10 to 12 minutes.

5. The people riding the bus on the "Park and Ride" service could be unloaded at one certain entrance. The loading after

church could also take place at the same door. This would insure that those riding would never be exposed to bad weather from the place they park until they enter the church building. This would be a real selling point. At the conclusion of the service, those who "Park and Ride" would simply come to the exit; and as soon as the bus was loaded, the people would be taken to their cars. This would be repeated until all were returned.

6. The city police could patrol the lots during the services to see that no cars parked in the "Park and Ride" lots were harmed.

7. This parking program could begin with a campaign to get a certain number of families to volunteer to "Park and Ride." This idea could be mentioned first to the leaders in order that they would be able to lead the way in this matter. The following card could be used to gain the signatures of those willing to participate.

Realizing the importance of every

part of the Lord's work and willing

to do all I can for the furtherance

of the Gospel -- I will

"PARK AND RIDE"

Signed_____ Family

There would be some minor details to work out as this program progressed, but they could be easily cared for.

Our People Are Joining Other Churches in the Suburbs

A large number of church members will continue to migrate further and further from the city. They leave the geographic area of the church. They shop near their new homes, and many of them send their children to schools near their homes;

but we want them to continue to attend the church that remains in the city.

A church program must be developed that makes the "drive worth the difference." People are interested in a ministry to the total family, and this is exactly what the downtown church must develop.

It is unnecessary to have people out to church or some church-related function every night of the week; but it is absolutely necessary to have as many meetings (such as deacons' meetings, finance committee meetings, teachers' and officers' meetings) as possible on Sundays and Wednesday nights. People would rather stay a little longer or come early for a meeting on Sunday and Wednesday than to come out another day of the week.

Our Members Live Everywhere

This can be made much, much more of an asset than it is a liability. It is true that there may be a community loyalty, and each member of the church might feel the urge to improve his own local community more than his desire to change the entire area; but at the same time, a church with a "citywide" vision must have people in every area surrounding the city proclaiming the Gospel to the entire city. Church members can be trained to win the lost in their own communities and bring these people with them to the downtown church.

Travel to and from the Church May Be Difficult

Unless a person living in the suburbs works in the city, he may not go into the area of the city for long periods of time. It may be difficult for him to find the church. Maps showing the direction to the church from any area surrounding the city should be given to each person visited by the church.

Visitation — Distance Must Be Dealt With

One common complaint of many visitation programs is the complaint of not having good prospects to visit. This, combined with the inability of those doing the visiting to find certain residential areas where better prospects live, makes it very necessary to work on this matter of people and places to visit. What can be done? Here are a few steps to take:

Let Us Find Out Where Our People Live

Certainly we realize that people can attend our church from any area where people are already coming to worship with us. By finding out where our own people live we can impress upon them the importance of being soul-conscious in their own neighborhood. We may also have doors opened to us in apartment complexes and mobile home parks where our people live that we did not realize.

Establish a Continual Search for Prospects

We can employ people to take census in certain areas systematically. The telephone can also be used to find prospects. Most important, every attempt must be made to make it convenient for our people to turn in names of those whom they know who need Christ. Every Christian must be made to realize his responsibility in this area.

We Must Attempt to Make More Distant
Residential Areas Seem Closer

In any city, population patterns change. People are constantly moving. A church located in or near the city may wake up one day to find that those who once attended the church faithfully when living in or around the same neighborhood have now moved to the suburbs and find it more convenient to attend a church in their new location. We must go to great lengths to convince our own people who are doing the visitation work that people will drive the distance from the suburbs to our church if they feel that the drive is worth what they find when they arrive. Anyone driving to employment or to shop in any area around our church during the week can also drive to our church to attend it faithfully.

Names of smaller towns and communities, along with streets, apartment complexes, and mobile home parks found in these areas should be given to those who will be visiting and also placed on the walls of the room where the visitation meeting is held.

Property, Buildings, and Space
Are Necessary to Reach People

Some caution must be taken in this area. Many downtown churches have operated large bus ministries and brought in great numbers of people. Space became a problem, so the church built for the bus crowd. This is a noble desire, but one fact was forgotten. The bus ministry is a mission endeavor, and bus children do not pay for buildings. Many well-meaning, Bible-believing pastors and churches have suffered because of overextending themselves financially. God help us to follow divine direction, live by faith—but to know the difference between faith and foolishness.

A church may be able to use old deserted buildings near its location until proper buildings can be erected. Also, the possibility of multiple services needs to be looked into. This is an idea to use the existing facilities more than one time on Sunday. This makes for maximum use of the church buildings.

The greatest opportunities for ministering to the lost multitudes of humanity lie at the doorstep of the downtown church. May God help us to turn every problem into an opportunity as we face this new frontier.

CHAPTER
10

Start New
Sunday Schools

"There is no birth without pain."

Extension Sunday Schools and Branch Sunday Schools

The New Testament Church has been commissioned to go after all people of all ages in all areas with the Gospel. Every local church should be committed to this task.

One proven method of reaching others is through the establishing of new Sunday Schools. These are preaching and teaching stations. This method of evangelism has proven to be very effective in the work of the Highland Park Baptist Church in Chattanooga, Tennessee.

THE NEW SUNDAY SCHOOLS
ARE DESPERATELY NEEDED

Broken Homes

The community without a Sunday School is a breeding ground for broken homes, juvenile delinquency, and all sorts of crime.

Soul-Winning Opportunities

New Sunday Schools provide soul-winning opportunities that go far beyond into areas where the clear gospel message has never been heard.

Reach Special Groups

Branch Sunday Schools help get the Gospel to multitudes of people who would not come to the main church. Remember, we must reach all people — all races — of all social standings.

They Grow Fast

New Sunday Schools grow faster and reach more people than old established Sunday Schools. This is also one big reason for continually establishing new classes in the main church.

People Need What They Cannot Provide for Themselves

Many people realize the need for a Bible-preaching station in their area but are financially unable to provide such a place. This is one reason for the mission-minded church that is already established to start a new Sunday School in the needy area.

Opportunity of Service

The branch Sunday School provides an excellent place to put church members to work.

Multitudes Are Not In Sunday School

Many millions of people in America are not in any Sunday School. Therefore, we must enroll them in new Sunday Schools.

STEPS IN STARTING THE NEW SUNDAY SCHOOLS

Without a determined commitment to reach all people, the new Sunday School will never get off the ground. Some may object because of finances; others may say there is no place to meet or no leadership. Still others may say that no branch work is needed because it would keep the present Sunday School from growing. This idea that branch Sunday Schools will keep the main work from growing is wrong. Just the opposite will be found to be true. The blessing of God will be upon this Sunday School for having a "mission heart."

Begin With A Burden

We must desire to obey Christ in reaching the unsaved and possess a genuine burden for all lost people.

Locate The Area

Find the area where people are in need of a Sunday School and do not have one. This may be a neglected rural area, a thickly populated inner city, or a special group of people that will not attend the present Sunday School.

Enlist and Train Leaders

The great need in the work of God is the need for laborers. When this need is met, all else seems to be simple. The Lord Jesus said we were to pray and ask God for laborers. (Luke 10:1-2) Enlist and train key people to carry on this work. In the beginning stages, this new Sunday School work could meet on Sunday afternoon, thus enabling workers in the sponsoring church to do "double duty" in working at both places. Dr. Max Helton is following this plan in the New York City area.

Find a Meeting Place

In most areas, a building can be found "rent free" or for just a small amount to begin the work. Perhaps a home could be used for a very short while. Think of every possible place that would be suitable that is not used during the time period you will want to conduct the service. Make a list of all the possibilities, and choose from this list as God leads and opens the door.

Set a Date to Begin the Sunday School

Allow yourself enough time to take care of all necessary plans, but do not just go on and on with plans — get started! Make a big day out of the first Sunday.

Publicize the Sunday School

Visit much in the area before the work starts. Use nicely printed material with time and place on it. Get names, phone numbers, and addresses of all those not presently attending a Sunday School faithfully; and work to get these present.

CHAPTER

11

Have an Afternoon Sunday School

"If we have the conviction that all people are lost, then we must also express the compassion to take the Gospel to all people."

A few weeks ago, one of the little boys that had just received Christ in our Afternoon Sunday School came up to his teacher and asked a puzzling question. He said, "Teacher, I just got saved and I know I am going to heaven. Does Jesus feed people in heaven?" The worker said, "Why do you ask such a question?" The little boy said, "Because I am hungry, and my daddy and mother are drunk and will not feed me." God help us to reach all people.

If we hold the conviction that the Lord Jesus Christ died for all people, and we must believe this, then we should have the compassion and determination to take the Gospel to all people. Often we have neglected to reach a certain element of people in our city.

Over one hundred years ago, the outstanding evangelist D. L. Moody became greatly concerned about reaching the neglected children in the city of Chicago. His burden led him to establish a Sunday Afternoon Sunday School that was used of God to reach thousands with the Gospel. This work later developed into the Moody Memorial Church. It was a new method of evangelism for his day, but it worked.

A few years ago, our pastor became greatly burdened to reach the neglected people of our city. Out of this burden grew the Sunday Afternoon Sunday School of our church. This ministry expresses our concern and commitment to see all people saved.

The Sunday School is conducted on Sunday Afternoon from 2:30 p.m. until 4:30 p.m. All the buildings and equipment of our church are used in this ministry. People of all ages are reached with the Gospel and taught the Word of God.

The vast majority of people attending this Sunday School ride our buses, but many also drive in. After the buses run on the morning routes, they return to the church, where a full crew of workers waits to take each bus to a certain area of the city to bring others who have been contacted and enlisted on Saturday.

Upon arriving at the church, the buses stop in front of the proper buildings for each age group. Before anyone is let off the bus, the bus workers are sure that each pupil has the number of the bus placed on his hand, along with a certain letter of the alphabet. The letter identifies the person with a particular geographical location of the city. This enables the pupil to attend a class with others from the same area of the city, even though the others may come on a different bus. This division of classes by geographical areas has proven to be of great benefit to the Sunday School teacher in his visitation of the pupils.

Everyone steps off the bus and enters into a preaching service geared to their particular age level. The preschool-age children go directly to a Sunday School class and do not attend any preaching assembly. They are dealt with about Christ very carefully on their level.

At the conclusion of the preaching time in each assembly, an invitation is given; and those responding are taken to a counseling room, where trained personal workers deal with them about being saved. After they are saved, they are taken to another large room and given instructions concerning obeying Christ in believer's baptism. If they know that Christ has saved them and they are willing to be baptized, they are taken to the baptistry room to prepare for baptism. Instruction and counseling are given at this time. After they are baptized, they return to the bus. The follow-up on these begins immediately.

Meanwhile, back in the assemblies, the invitation has been concluded; and the remaining pupils are dismissed into classes by geographical locations. The teachers of these pupils have attended four training sessions dealing with presenting the Gospel, the use of literature and visual aids, room arrangements, and discipline. At 4:30 p.m., the classes are dismissed; and the pupils return to the buses.

Hundreds and hundreds are coming to know Christ through this ministry. Many have answered the call to full-time Christian service; branch Sunday Schools and chapels have been started; and a preparatory Bible Institute has begun. Lift up your eyes and look on the fields, they are white already to harvest. Reach all people with the Gospel using every available means and method to get the job done.

12

Begin an Adult Advance

"Everything rises or falls on leadership."
Dr. Lee Roberson

The greatest failure and embarrassment of fundamental work in America is our failure to reach adults.

The Church Is Suffering From:
1. **Lack of Leadership**
2. **Little Finances**
3. **Lagging Influence Upon the Community**
4. **Failure to Reach the Entire Home**

Any church that can break the barriers in reaching adults is headed toward its greatest days.

Just a few weeks ago, a Russian immigrant and his family were contacted by one of the men of our church. After a brief conversation, the man discovered that this gentleman, his wife, and daughter were unsaved. He took his Bible in hand and led them to a saving knowledge of the Lord Jesus Christ. They came forward the next Sunday and made public their profession of faith and followed the Lord in baptism. The Lord brought that man from the other side of the world in order for him to hear the Gospel. It was so thrilling to see each of them trusting Christ as Savior. This story could be repeated time and time again of families in our churches. We must reach moms and dads.

There are over 100 million adults in America not enrolled in Sunday School.

Eighty-five percent of all our prospects for Sunday School are adults. This means that our churches should be spending a great deal of their time reaching adults, but in most cases this is not being done. The challenge of reaching adults in America has been neglected.

We are afraid of offending those we already have and are negligent in attempting to reach those outside the four walls of our buildings. As a result of this, we find one of the following:

A group of old established classes, which have become pockets of poison, meeting in plush classrooms they call "their room," taught by someone preparing a stale lecture to the same little group each week that has lost all purpose and vision of what an adult class should be doing.

Or you find a large room (most of the time the auditorium) filled with adults being taught by one person. This arrangement may look good at the start; but it fails in the selection, training, and motivation of new adult leadership to start new classes reaching unsaved adults. Sometimes this type of class is nothing more than another little worship service.

ADULT PROSPECTS ARE OUT THERE

We must:

1. Enroll them in Bible study.
2. Lead them to Christ.
3. Involve them in all the life of the church.

How Can This Be Done?

Locate adult prospects.

Select and train teachers and leaders for new adult classes.

Locate space to begin new adult classes.

Organize the new classes.

Go after adults, using the best methods available to enroll them in the Bible study classes.

CHAPTER

13

Have a Teachers' and Officers' Meeting

> *"It is not as important to whom we teach as it is for whom we teach."*
>
> Dr. J. R. Faulkner

The meeting should begin with a good song followed by a brief prayer. Reports of the previous week should be given, and then the lesson material should be presented. Recognize anyone who needs to be recognized, and place emphasis where it is needed. The pastor and any other special speaker will stir each worker to do his best. Plans for the future need to be introduced, and any teaching helps available should be given. The Sunday School teachers' and officers' meeting does for the Sunday School the following things.

It Helps Us Gain a Vision of the Entire Work.

It Causes Us to See the Place of Each Individual As Far As His Task Is Concerned.

In other words, we are telling people, "You are important. What you do is essential." When we have a teachers' meeting, we have workers and pupils to attend also.

It Improves the Work of Our Sunday School.

It Provides Fellowship, Inspiration, Information, and Instruction.

It is not enough just to throw out information about things to do. We must show people how to apply these things. It is not enough to tell them we have visualized songs they can use. Show them how to use it. It is not enough to say, "Here is a great idea. Let me give it to you." Show them how to apply it. Instruct them.

Teachers' and Officers' meeting of Highland Park Baptist Church.

The Meeting Is to Encourage Prayer.

It is not necessary to spend long periods in prayer. Very little is accomplished sometimes in public prayer meetings as far as prayer is concerned. The greatest thing is not the praying that is done there but the encouragement to pray once one leaves the meeting.

It Promotes Visitation.

The Meeting Helps to Solve Problems.

We may have, sometimes, in the Sunday School, a certain individual who is constantly having problems. If we are not careful, letting that person speak each time will drag the meeting down. Never let people speak openly in the meeting unless they have been asked to speak for fear that some deadhead will get up.

It Prepares Workers.

Giving of teaching materials and this type of thing can be done.

It Helps to Place Emphasis Where Emphasis Is Needed.

We do not emphasize the same thing every week. There are certain things that go wrong and emphasis needs to be placed on these things. Meeting regularly helps us to place the emphasis where it is needed.

**It Helps You to Recognize Those
Who Have Done an Outstanding Job.**

It gives an opportunity to give reports. Have a report every week. Prepare a report of the work.

It Helps You to Set Goals.

It Keeps People Stirred and Challenged.

14

Departmentalize Your Sunday School

"There is no victory without a battle."

A good Sunday School is not an accident. One must realize what is involved in the building of a Sunday School and be willing to pay the price to see the plan carried out.

One important step in the building of a Sunday School is this matter of departmentalization. The day is past when everyone goes to one large room and is taught together. The departmentalized Sunday School operates so much more effectively. Progressive Sunday Schools everywhere use the idea of departmentalization.

It is understood that the Sunday School should meet the needs of pupils — physically, mentally, socially, and spiritually. However, the first three of these needs are dealt with in order to meet the fourth — the spiritual need. The basis for departmentalizing a Sunday School is to do the best job possible of meeting this need. Most people of the same age face the same spiritual needs. Therefore, the best method of departmentalizing a Sunday School is not by scholarship or environment but by age.

REASONS FOR DEPARTMENTALIZATION

1. **It Increases Effectiveness In Evangelism.** It makes it easier to assign the responsibility of reaching a certain age group to certain leaders.
2. **It Provides A Better Teaching Environment.** The teacher has a big task at best; but by teaching pupils of the same age, the teacher can do a better job.
3. **It Encourages Pupils To Invite Friends.** Children of the same age and school grade usually run together. The pupil can feel more at ease inviting his friends to Sunday School when he knows they will be in his class.

DIFFICULTIES IN DEPARTMENTALIZATION

1. **Misunderstanding Of The Plan** The system of departmentalizing the Sunday School is a plan to make certain age divisions that will enable everyone to do a better job.

2. **Teachers Desire To Keep Their Pupils** If this were done in every class, there would soon develop a stagnant condition in the Sunday School. The desire should be to do the best for each pupil and to reach the unsaved — not to just seek to please a teacher.

3. **Overcautiousness About Offending Others** The attitude of "let well enough alone" has stifled growth in many areas of the Lord's work. It is possible to have a departmentalized Sunday School and also to provide special classes for certain groups.

HELPFUL HINTS IN MAKING AGE DIVISIONS IN THE SUNDAY SCHOOL

As mentioned already, there are reasons for and against the departmentalization of Sunday School classes. The evidence of growing Sunday Schools across America points to a definite advantage for strict age divisions combined with some special classes. Among adults one will find in many great Sunday Schools a combination of classes with strict age division, along with other classes that are somewhat of "catchalls" for any adult that wishes to study the Bible. There is a definite advantage to this as long as the classes continue to grow.

1. **Inform The Leaders Of The Plan.** Let them know it is being done to reach more of the unsaved community.

2. **Have An Annual Promotion Day.** This allows an opportunity to show progress and keep the Sunday School moving and growing.

3. **Use Geographical Divisions Within The Age Division.** If your church is located in a city situation, it will be necessary as it grows to have more than one class for a certain age. The classes can be divided by geographical sections. This makes it much easier for the teacher to visit the unsaved of his age group for his class and also is a definite advantage in visiting class members.

4. **As The Sunday School Grows** it will be necessary to have an Associate Superintendent over each department.

The following are varied ideas on departments and divisions in the Sunday School:

Simple Sunday School Divisions

Titles	Age
Nursery Division	3 years and under
Preschool Division	4 and 5-year-olds
Children's Division	6 through 12-year-olds
Youth Division	13 through 18-year-olds
Adult Division	19 and up

Standard Sunday School Departments

Titles	Age
Nursery Department	3 years and under
Beginner Department	4 through 5-year-olds
Primary Department	6 through 8-year-olds
Junior Department	9 through 12-year-olds
Intermediate Department	13 through 15-year-olds
Youth Department	16 through 18-year-olds
Adult Department	19 and up
Special Department	Deaf, Retarded, and Foreign Language

Divisions Using Grades

Titles	Age
Nursery	3 years and under
Preschool	Kindergarten
First grade	Grade one
Second grade	Grade two
Third grade	Grade three
Fourth grade	Grade four
Fifth grade	Grade five
Sixth grade	Grade six
Junior High	Grades seven and eight
Senior High	Grades nine through twelve
College	College students
Adults	19 and up

Another variation of Children's Departments

Titles	Age
Children A	First and second grade
Children B	Third and fourth grade
Children C	Fifth and sixth grade

Another variation of Children's Departments

Titles	Age
Younger Children	Ages 6-7
Middle Children	Ages 8-9
Older Children	Ages 10-11

Another variation of Youth Departments

Titles	Age
Pre-Teen	Ages 11-12
Young Teens	Ages 13-14
Mid-Teens	Ages 14-15
Older Teens	Ages 16-18

Another variation of Adult Classes and Departments

Titles	Age
College and Career	College age
Single Adults	Usually younger adults
Young Adults	18-25
Adults	25-40
Median Adults	40-55
Older Adults	55-65
Retired Adult Class	65 and up

15

Use These Notes and Ideas For Effectiveness In Departments

"Successful servants of the Lord do not reach plateaus; they climb mountains."

by J. R. Faulkner

Specific Notes and Ideas for the Cradle Roll Department or Nursery

(Infants through three-year-old children)

1. The nursery and/or Cradle Roll Department should be bright, cheerful, and colorful. Do *not* paint it white. White paint reminds the child of his last visit to the doctor or local hospital. The nursery workers should also be dressed in pastels — *not white*. Decorate walls with color and, if possible, with Bible characters and scenes.

2. Have adult classes turn in names of parents who have new babies.

3. Make personal visit to the hospital at birth of a baby — or to the home as soon as possible.

4. Enroll new babies in the Cradle Roll Department even before they come to church. Make out a certificate for the family, and enter the child's name on records so the family can receive your mail. Place the baby on the permanent roll once the child has been brought to the nursery.

5. Gifts may be given to new babies. Some churches do; some do not. But each child should receive a certificate which can be framed.

6. Visit young mothers to encourage them. Try to show the value of the church nursery, and urge them to use it.

7. If the nursery is handled properly, it can be used to reach many unsaved parents for Christ. You gain their interest when you show interest in their little ones.

**Specific Notes and Ideas for the
Beginner and Primary Departments**

(Beginners ages 4 and 5; primaries ages 6-8)

1. Beginner and primary-age children respond readily to many incentives. One is "ribbon collection." Mail a different color ribbon each week for a given number of weeks (4 or 8) to the children. Ask them to bring the ribbon to Sunday School on Sunday and match it with one of the same color tied to a chair. Award all who bring their ribbon. At end of the month or eight weeks, award all who saved all ribbons (100 percent).

2. Another incentive is the *"birthday cake."* All young children respond to this. Have a birthday cake (dummy) each Sunday. Put a candle on it for each one having a birthday that week. Let them blow out the candles. A birthday present with different color ribbon for boys and girls may be kept in a beautifully decorated box. Let them choose one.

   Recognize birthdays in a special way. Have those who had birthdays in the preceding week to sit in a special birthday chair. Use the cake idea and present a gift.

3. Prepare a well-planned pre-Sunday School table, using puzzles, pictures to color, and books for the beginner and primary children to enjoy. This keeps interest until Sunday School begins.

4. Make personal visits to each new child enrolled to encourage attendance.

5. Reward children — always — for bringing visitors.

6. Have an Honor Roll each month. On first Sunday, have all children stand who were present each Sunday in the preceding month. Give each a small gift.

7. Give a nice New Testament on Easter Sunday to each child who has a perfect Sunday School attendance record from January 1 through Easter.

8. Mail a weekly letter to children, giving plans for next Sunday. Include a picture to be colored and returned on Sunday. Reward them for this.

9. In your mailing, send an outline of animals, Bible characters, or biblical scenes, which they are to color and identify and bring to class on the following Sunday. Give an award for best work.

10. Plan programs to include the children. Let them take part by singing and quoting Scripture.

11. Use flannelgraph, object lessons, and other forms of visual aid equipment.

12. Teach beginners and primaries to give to missions by having

"Pete the Pig" piggy bank for missions. Let them bring pennies or nickels to "feed" the pig each Sunday.

13. Use "mystery chairs" in class each Sunday. Before the children arrive, select two or three chairs by number to be mystery chairs for the day. Place the numbers under a seal on the bulletin board. At a given time, remove the seal to reveal the numbers of the mystery chairs. Reward children seated in those chairs.

14. In the Primary Department, on a given Sunday each year, you may have a "Queen for a Day." Let the children vote by ballot who will be queen for that day. Place a little crown on her head, and let her sit in a special, decorated chair. Present gifts.

On the following Sunday, you could have a "King for a Day." Follow the same procedure.

Specific Notes and Ideas for the Junior Department

(children ages 9-12)

1. Junior-age youngsters may respond to the incentive of the *"grab box."* When a child brings one visitor, he and his visitor are given an opportunity to take one gift from the grab box. There should be one big gift (silver dollar, etc.) in the box and many smaller gifts — beautifully wrapped.

2. *Certificates* with attendance stars are good to inspire faithful attendance of juniors. Stars are placed on the certificates each Sunday the child is present. It is presented to the child at the end of the quarter.

3. *Attendance charts* may be used with stars by children's names to record attendance. Colored stars are used to denote attendance, memory work, visitors brought, etc.

4. All types of contests may be conducted in the Junior Department. Some may run for a three-month period. Points are given for attendance, bringing of visitors, attendance to services of main church, Bible reading, memory work, and bringing Bible to Sunday School. Winners are rewarded with gifts, trips and outings.

5. *Memory work chart* Junior-age children may be given a slip of paper each Sunday with a verse and reference on it, which he is challenged to memorize for the next Sunday. Stars may be placed by the child's name to indicate his or her progress.

One teacher used a large red heart with the Scripture verse Psalm 119:11 printed on it. Each child's name was typed on a small white heart, which was tacked to a large red one. Each Sunday when a child had satisfactorily quoted his memory verse, his slip of paper with the verse on it was slipped behind the white heart. At the end of the quarter, the child with the best memory work record was rewarded.

6. Use the jigsaw puzzle idea — puzzle pieces are mimeographed on back of letter to class. Cards are cut in half in "puzzle form." One end is given to all class members who attend the Officer's and Teacher's Meeting on Wednesday evening. The members bring the puzzle piece to class Sunday and receive a gift if their puzzle piece matches the other end of any of the few puzzle pieces shown on the back of the mimeographed letter sent to members that week.

Specific Notes and Ideas for the Intermediate Department

(children ages 13-16)

1. Each new year might be started by naming "Mr. and Miss Intermediate." These are chosen by popular vote, with Christian character, testimony, faithfulness to all church services, and all-around personality as the criteria.

   These young people are to lead class activities for the year ahead. Promotion and elimination is done in the month of January, with final voting on the first Sunday in February.

2. "Intermediate Day" always attracts great interest. All of the program is handled by the youth themselves — special music, testimonies, prayer, Bible reading, and the teaching of the classes. Those to teach are chosen by the superintendent.

3. Since most promotion is done in the department and not in the individual classes, oftentimes outside people are brought in to provide a program. Chalk artists, magicians, karatists, musicians, etc. may be used. Sports stars with good testimonies may be used here also.

4. If you have a junior high or high school group, you may wish to have someone keep up with their football and basketball schedule. Build mailing lists of all players. Write them before each major game — cheer them on. If they win, follow it up with a congratulatory note, praising them. This done consistently will build friends.

5. Older intermediates (ages 15-16) like to have a king and queen chosen for the department. They select a young man and a young lady to reign for a year. They are chosen by popular vote. Very high standards of faithfulness are required for eligibility for this honor. These standards are known to all and are to be observed when choices are made.

16

Put a Sunday School Secretary to Work

"Unless I help someone I have failed."
Dr. Lee Roberson

As a Sunday School grows, it will become necessary to enlist and train someone to perform the duties of a Sunday School secretary. At the beginning, this may be a volunteer or volunteers until the work warrants the hiring of a paid employee working full-time at this job.

The normal requirements looked for in a secretary will be needed in this person. This is, of course, a ministry where the highest of Christian courtesy and character must prevail. The particular responsibilities will be as follows.

Assist the Sunday School Superintendent

This secretary must seek to aid the Sunday School superintendent in any area of the work to make his job easier.

Be a Help to Each Sunday School Class

The Sunday School secretary must seek to make it easier for each class to be active. Prepare the Sunday School reports (attendance, averages, etc.). Keep a record of those enrolled and the new members of each class.

Prepare the Sunday School Outline

In our church, Dr. Cliff Robinson prepares the Sunday School outline for the teachers; and the secretary mimeographs the outline in order for copies to be handed out.

Handle Sunday School Mailing

Type and mimeograph Sunday School class letters and newsletters. She must also acquaint everyone with the rules and procedures in bulk mailing.

Miss Mildred Eifert, secretary to Dr. J.R. Faulkner, has done a masterful job of keeping up with every phase of church and school development including the Sunday School.

Type a List of Sick and Bereaved Members

Each class has a card on which to place the names and addresses of class members that are sick or bereaved. From these cards a list is prepared and given to the pastor for visitation.

Lend a Hand in Special Class Projects

When the Sunday School or some class of the Sunday School has a party or banquet, the secretary is willing to help in any way possible.

Sort and Deposit Bulk Mail

Each class sending a class letter must turn the letter in ready for mailing by a certain date. The Sunday School secretary sorts the mail by zip code and deposits it in the mail bag for the postman.

Fix Address Systems for Classes

A class doing a mailing each week can benefit greatly from having addresses of class members placed on an addressograph or mimeographed on address labels. The Sunday School secretary handles this.

Type Absentee Lists for Classes to Follow Up

Every Sunday School class has a roll card filled out on each class member. These cards are placed in a 3 x 5 box, and the roll is checked on these cards each Sunday. The box is returned to the Sunday School office, and a list of absentees is prepared for visitation.

Provide Sunday School Supplies

The secretary keeps supplies for classes (record books, promotion certificates, etc.).

Keep Up With Correspondence

There is a great deal of correspondence in connection with the Sunday School work. Letters are received requesting information on our Sunday School, and these letters must be answered. Orders for materials must be placed, thank-you notes must be mailed, congratulation wishes must be sent and a number of other types of correspondence must be taken care of.

Prepare Sample Packets of Sunday School Materials

As requests for information increase, it becomes very necessary to have packets of material ready to hand inquirers.

Order Sunday School Literature

Most of the materials and literature for our Sunday School are prepared by our own people. Of course, there are certain visual aids and literature orders for younger children that must be placed.

17

Keep Records and Use Forms

"Do what is right whether you feel like it or not."

A system of records in any Sunday School is an absolute must. So many facets of the work depend a great deal on accurate records. Some may argue that record-keeping is too expensive, others state that it is very time-consuming, while a few may even refuse to keep records because of the so-called "red tape." The truth remains that a Sunday School cannot function properly without good record-keeping.

A Sunday School teacher that does not keep accurate records does not plan to do his best and has no intentions of helping each particular individual who needs to be ministered to by his class. Every teacher should at least begin with an up-to-date roll book. This book, among many other things, serves as a prayer list for the teacher.

A preacher recently related a humorous story about two farmers in the state of Georgia. One farmer sold the other one two mules. Within a week's time, the buyer of the mules called the man that sold them to him and said, "Those mules you sold me just died." The other fellow replied, "Well I'll say, they never did that before!"

Some Sunday School workers say, "We have never kept records before. Why start now?" Because records aid in doing a better job for Christ in the Sunday School. The following forms can be used in the Sunday School.

The following must be filled out and approved by the pastor and church.

APPLICATION FOR POSITION AS TEACHER
HIGHLAND PARK BAPTIST SUNDAY SCHOOL

NAME (in full) _____

ADDRESS _____ PHONE _____

Do you know that you are a child of God? _____

How long a member of Highland Park Baptist Church? _____

List any other office now held in church _____

Have you ever taught in a Sunday School before? ____ Where? _____

_____ Age and sex of pupils _____

If approved as a teacher, do you have a definite assignment? ____

DEPARTMENT _____ CLASS _____

**DO YOU NOW PLEDGE TO ATTEND THE FOLLOWING MEETINGS UNLESS YOU
ARE HINDERED BY GOOD AND SUFFICIENT REASON:** Sunday morning
service, Sunday evening service, Teachers' and Officers' Meeting, Prayer service (Wednesday)? YES _____ NO _____

Do you understand that you are to engage in weekly visitation,
preferably on Thursday nights? _____

IS IT YOUR PURPOSE TO LIVE A CONSECRATED CHRISTIAN LIFE SO AS
TO REFLECT CREDIT ON THE WORK OF THIS SUNDAY SCHOOL? _____

Is it your purpose to give your full cooperation to the leaders
of the church and Sunday School? _____

                              SIGNED _____

APPROVED BY DEPT. SUPT. _____

APPROVED BY GEN. SUPT. _____

ELECTED _____

52

This is a permanent Sunday School enrollment card filled out on each Sunday School pupil.

Name_____Phone_____

Street & No._____

City_____Group No._____

SUNDAY	(1)	(2)	(3)	(4)	(5)	SUNDAY	(1)	(2)	(3)	(4)	(5)
OCT.	( )	( )	( )	( )	( )	APR.	( )	( )	( )	( )	( )
NOV.	( )	( )	( )	( )	( )	MAY	( )	( )	( )	( )	( )
DEC.	( )	( )	( )	( )	( )	JUNE	( )	( )	( )	( )	( )
JAN.	( )	( )	( )	( )	( )	JULY	( )	( )	( )	( )	( )
FEB.	( )	( )	( )	( )	( )	AUG.	( )	( )	( )	( )	( )
MAR.	( )	( )	( )	( )	( )	SEPT.	( )	( )	( )	( )	( )

This certificate is presented to our teachers after attending a training course in the work of the Afternoon Sunday School. Something similar to this could be used in all Sunday Schools.

TEACHER TRAINING COURSE

AWARDED TO

_____

CERTIFICATE   OF AWARD

For satisfactorily completing
the Afternoon Sunday School
Teacher Training Course of the
Highland Park Baptist Church.

Pastor

The names of all sick and bereaved class members are placed on this card and returned to the Sunday School office. From this a list is prepared for the Pastor.

SICK LIST FOR WEDNESDAY PRAYER SERVICE

Class_____Date_____

Report Given By_____Phone_____

Full Name: Mr., Mrs., or Miss If Adult	Address	Our Church Member Yes No		Remarks

This Card Will Be Picked Up By Your Associate Superintendent.

A drop card like this is filled out on a pupil for one of three reasons — death, moving to another city, joining another church.

DROP CARD

NAME_____

ADDRESS_____

CLASS_____

REASON_____

DATE_____

Signed_____

Please return this card to the Sunday School Office.

This card is designed to register all visitors and then used to correspond with them.

```
┌─────────────────────────────────────────────────┐
│                 VISITOR  CARD                     │
│                                                   │
│   NAME_____    │
│                                                   │
│   ADDRESS_____   │
│                                                   │
│   CITY_____STATE____       │
│                                                   │
│   ZIP CODE _____PHONE____       │
│                                                   │
│   GUEST OF_____    │
│                                                   │
│   DATE_____    │
│           This card for records                   │
└─────────────────────────────────────────────────┘
```

This card is filled out on all new members and returned to the Sunday School Office.

```
┌─────────────────────────────────────────────────┐
│                                                   │
│                                                   │
│               NEW  MEMBERS                        │
│                                                   │
│    NAME_____     │
│                                                   │
│    ADDRESS_____     │
│                                          (if child)│
│    CLASS/DEPT._____ AGE_____        │
│                                                   │
│    PHONE_____DATE_____        │
│                                  mo/day/yr         │
│    Please return this card to the Sunday School Office.│
│                                                   │
└─────────────────────────────────────────────────┘
```

This is a work sheet used by the Sunday School secretary to prepare the Sunday School report.

GENERAL SECRETARY'S REPORT   DATE_____   WEATHER_____

SPECIAL DAY:

	ENR	NEW MEM	GOAL	ATTN	AVG ATT	VTRS	T&O GOAL	T&O ATTN
GENERAL OFFICERS								
DIVISION 1 - Hammel								
FRIENDSHIP CLASS								
JOY CLASS								
GRACE CLASS								
MEN'S CLASS								
TABERNACLE CLASS								
SUNDAY SCHOOL II								
SUNDAY SCHOOL III								
TOTALS								
DIVISION 2 - Clonts								
CRADLE ROLL DEPT.								
BEGINNER A DEPT.								
BEGINNER B DEPT.								
PRIMARY A DEPT.								
PRIMARY B DEPT.								
PRIMARY C DEPT.								
TOTALS								
DIVISION 3 - Wilson								
JUNIOR A DEPT.								
JUNIOR B DEPT.								
JUNIOR C DEPT.								
JUNIOR D DEPT.								
YOUNG TEENS DEPT.								
MID-TEENS DEPT.								
TEENS FOR CHRIST DEPT.								
CHURCH YOUTH DEPT.								
YOUTH FELLOWSHIP DEPT.								
TOTALS								
DIVISION 4 - Lockery								
HELPING HANDS CLASS								
SCOTT CLASS								
PHILATHEA								
RADIO BIBLE CLASS								
FAITH FELLOWSHIP CLASS								
MARANATHA CLASS								
BUSINESS WOMEN'S CLASS								
SPANISH-SPEAKING CLASS								
OPEN DOOR BIBLE CLASS								
ADULT BIBLE CLASS								
TOTALS								
DIVISION 5 - Beckner								
COUPLES FOR CHRIST CLASS								
SILENT MEN'S CLASS								
PROCLAIMERS OF CHRIST								
SILENT SHEPHERD CLASS								
SEEKERS CLASS								
TEMPLE BIBLE CLASS								
EBENEZER CLASS								
WHOSOEVER WILL CLASS								
HASKELL CLASS								
COLLEGE & CAREER CLASS								
COLLEGE GIRLS								
TOTALS								
MAIN SCHOOL TOTALS								
CHAPELS								
GRAND TOTALS								

A. M. BUSES   _____

S. S. II   _____

TOTAL   _____

All the Sunday School offering and new member, drop, and visitors cards are placed inside this envelope. The class report is given on the outside.

DIVISION_____

Name_____

Date_____

ENROLLMENT_____

New Members +_____

Drop   -_____

NEW ENROLLMENT_____

Visitors_____

ATTENDANCE

THIS SPACE IS FOR ANY MESSAGES TO THE
SUNDAY SCHOOL SECRETARY

This letter is sent to each new person attending the Sunday School class.

Highland Park
BAPTIST
CHURCH

1901 UNION AVENUE • CHATTANOOGA, TENNESSEE 37404 • PHONE 615/698-6021

PASTORS
LEE ROBERSON, D. D.
J. R. FAULKNER, L. L. D

Miss Jeanine Smith
1504 Union Avenue
Chattanooga, Tennessee   37404

Dear Friend,

We were so happy to have you in the class Sunday. I hope the Bible
Study was a blessing to you. It is our desire to help people.

The most important matter in all the world is your relationship to
the Lord Jesus. Enclosed is some material you will enjoy
reading. See you in the class next Sunday.

Sincerely,

Clarence Sexton

Clarence Sexton
Philippians 4:19

CS/js

Enclosures:2

CAMP JOY   —   WORLD WIDE FAITH MISSIONS   —   TENNESSEE TEMPLE SCHOOLS

"GOSPEL DYNAMITE" DAILY BROADCAST—BRANCH CHURCHES— UNION GOSPEL MISSION

"THE EVANGELIST" BI-WEEKLY PAPER—SUNDAY SCHOOL BUSES

CHAPTER

18

Have Standards for Teachers and Officers

"The secret to power in the Christian life is Biblical separation."

It is evident that many Sunday Schools fail and many suffer because of poor teachers and poor teaching. Definite standards for all teachers and officers who are elected by the church will help to remedy this situation.

The following four standards, if adhered to, will increase the efficiency and depth of our work:

I. **SALVATION.** Every teacher should give definite evidence of salvation and should state that he knows that he is saved before accepting a position of work in the Sunday School.   I have discovered that in some Sunday Schools unsaved people are used as officers. (It seems to be a common practice in some places for non-church members to take positions of leadership in the church).

II. **FAITHFULNESS.** Every teacher should be required to sign a pledge to attend the following services: Sunday morning, Sunday evening, and the midweek prayer service, plus the teachers' and officers' meeting on Wednesday if the church has one. Faithful church attendance will mean growth in grace, better working relationship with the pastor and the church at large, and will provide a good example for others.

III. **SEPARATION.** Every teacher and Sunday School leader should agree to abstain from all appearance of evil. Separation from the world should be interpreted by the pastor and accepted by all leaders. The definition of separation may vary in different parts of the country.

IV. **LOYALTY.** Every teacher and officer should state that he will give loyal support to the church, the pastor, and the general program of the local church. Disloyalty is a sin. The Sunday School will grow if there is a spirit of loyalty to the entire work.

CHAPTER
19

Get the Best Job
Out of Your Teachers

"Your example is more powerful than your teaching.

Dr. J. R. Faulkner

Every pastor or Sunday School superintendent wants to get the best out of the workers who work in his Sunday School. These are some ideas about how to get the best out of the people who work. If we are not careful, we are doing just the same thing all of the time.

This is one-on-one with your teachers. How are we going to get them to do a better job? How are we going to get them to do the best job they can do? How are we going to be the leaders we should be and bring the best out of them?

ENCOURAGE THEM TO RISE ABOVE
ALL THAT HAS BEEN DONE IN THE PAST

Do a little research. How many have they had in their class? What is the most they have had? Are they seeing people saved? What is the best job that has been done in Bible memory? How many of the pupils know the books of the Bible? This is the type thing we mean. Do more than has been done in the past. Rise above. Reach new goals. Here is the thing again of frontier and adventure. Do we realize there are a lot of preachers across America whose ministries are just nominal because they have gotten content with settling down Sunday after Sunday, week after week, to the same old thing. Never get in that rut. Do we want our lives to count for God to the fullest? Do we want to reach every soul that can be reached? Do we want to train everybody we can train? Do we wish to excel in the work of God? We are not talking about pride. We are talking about being all we can be for God and His glory. Stir everybody that can be stirred for God. Reach everybody that can be reached for God. There is a frontier and adventure and challenge to that.

PROVIDE NECESSARY MATERIALS FOR IMPROVEMENT

Encourage them to do more than has ever been done before, but do not get them all enthused and let them hang. Give them what they need to get the job done. Do they need a helper? Do they need better visuals? Do they need other materials? Do they need a little training in songs? What do they need? Provide it for them. That is your job.

GET THE TEACHER TO SET GOALS
FOR HIMSELF AND HIS CLASS

Notice how that was worded. I did not say, "Get the teacher's goals to him." I said, "Get the teacher to set goals." Goals are more often reached when they are not handed out to people but when people determine what their own goals are going to be. We will do a more effective job on buses, in Sunday School, in soul winning, and in everything else if we will say to people, "You pray about what God wants you to do — the goal you need to set for yourself." Do not just give them a goal. Let them set it. Get that person to set goals for himself and for his class.

TAKE A REGULAR CHECK-UP ON THE CLASS

Imagine one has a certain goal out here to reach, a certain number that he intends to have. On the way to that mountain, there are hills to go over and to cross. We must enroll people. Enlarge the organization. Take a check-up. Have we crossed this hill? Have we gotten over this hill? Do not just stand back here and wait for the man to conquer the mountain. Take a check-up on things.

ALLOW THE TEACHER TO EXCEL
IN THE AREAS HE IS STRONGEST, AND
TEACH HIM TO SEEK HELP IN HIS WEAK AREAS

Everyone can excel in some things and is weak in others. One of the big hindrances to lots of pastors is the fact that they will not have a secretary or an assistant. They could do many times what they are doing if they would just get other people involved. Sometimes if they do get a man they give him no liberty to work. That is the wrong thing to do. We must provide guidelines and a framework in which to work, yet let that individual excel and give him a certain amount of liberty and freedom. As he proves himself, he can be given more liberty and more freedom. Observe him — where he needs help, help him. We get much more done in the work of God if we do not care who gets the credit for doing it.

KEEP THE LINES OF COMMUNICATION OPEN

Do not get them closed. A person has to be able to talk to his supervisor, and his supervisors must be able to talk with him.

20

Have a Space Probe

> "Discouragers always overstate their problems."
>
> Dr. Fred Afman

Determine to find every available space to have a Sunday School class. Many surprises will come when a probe for space is started.

LIST ALL EMPTY ROOMS

Make a list of every room, every closet, and every office that is not being used during the Sunday School time at 9:45 a.m. This does not mean that every room on this list will be used for a class, but it will allow one to see what is available.

MAKE THE BEST USE OF SPACE ALREADY OCCUPIED

Find rooms that are not used to the fullest. Attempting to shift people from one location to another can be a dangerous business. Many do not like to move, but there are some classes and perhaps even departments occupying space they do not plan to ever fill. Be careful to base all the relocating on the opportunity to win souls. Some have a large room that will accommodate 300 and have never exceeded 30. Better use of this valuable space can be made. One church had a class of men averaging around five or six a Sunday meeting in the auditorium. This class was relocated and a new adult class begun in the auditorium that exceeded over one hundred per Sunday.

THINK ABOUT SUNDAY SCHOOLS
AT A DIFFERENT TIME PERIOD

Over one hundred years ago, D. L. Moody built one of the greatest Sunday Schools in America on Sunday afternoon at 3:00. This Sunday School later became the Moody Memorial Church. At Highland Park we have started a second Sunday

School presently averaging over 1,500 each week. This Sunday School is able to utilize all our present facilities at 2:30 on Sunday afternoon. We are getting maximum use from every building and classroom through this double use.

CHAPTER

21

Have an Annual Promotion Day

> *"The greatest knowledge is the will of God. The greatest success is to do the will of God."*
>
> George W. Truett

There are many important days in the life of a Sunday School, and one of the most important of these is "Promotion Day." This is a must for a growing Sunday School. This big day grows out of the need of the Sunday School to advance.

Promotion Day marks the end of one educational year in a church and the beginning of another. In most churches, the educational year begins on the first Sunday in October. This means that the promotion can actually take place on the last Sunday in September, thus enabling a fresh start for the new year.

The purpose of this day is not only to recognize and promote those who have been faithful throughout the year, but also to round up those who have been absent. It acquaints the pupils with their new teacher and class location.

So much action and movement on this day will produce a great deal of confusion unless careful plans are made. The final part of the class period on the Sunday before the new educational year begins should be used for actual promotion time.

The pupils should receive a personal escort to their new class and department. Proper introductions and records should be given to the new teachers and department superintendents. Before the pupils are promoted and taken from their old class, recognition should be given to those to whom it is due . Also, a list of those being promoted should be read. A certificate like the following should be presented to each pupil being promoted on Promotion Day.

CHAPTER

22

Use the Mail

"Use every available means to reach every available person."

1. Keep an up-to-date mailing list of all your people, and add to it as often as possible.

2. Design your own telegraph blank and envelope to send announcements of up-coming events.

3. Mail weekly letters to your regular constituents, giving full announcements of coming events. Urge them to pray, witness, and to invite folk to your church.

4. Follow up new contacts with a personal letter; and visit, when possible, during the week following their initial visit to your church — the sooner the better.

5. When writing a personal letter, save the most important points for a postscript on your letter. It will always be read.

6. For something different, try a letter in script — using a flair pen; and vary the colors.

7. Vary the size of your mailing piece as well as the color and design. One week you might use a large card or envelope — the next, a small one. Sameness soon becomes monotonous.

8. In your class, prepare a mailing list of the families of class members, listing all birthdays, anniversaries, wedding dates, etc. Have the class mail beautiful cards each Sunday if the event falls in the coming week.

9. Mail out Bible crossword puzzles to members of your class. Offer awards for the correct solutions.

10. As you send mail, letters, cards, announcements, etc. to your class each week, urge class members to make scrapbooks or to keep copies of all you send plus the bulletins from the morning service. Give three handsome awards at the end of the year to the three persons who have the best and most complete collections. — *J. R. Faulkner*

CHAPTER
23

Plan A Sunday School Campaign

> *"Attempt great things for God – expect great things from God."*
> William Carey

"During this campaign, we shall have more in Sunday School, see more people saved and baptized, have larger offerings, and give more to missions than at any other time in our church's history." The preceding statement can be true in the life of a church if necessary plans are made and God's people are willing to trust Him for the victory. The following steps should be taken.

SEEK THE LORD'S DIRECTION IN EVERY PART OF THE SUNDAY SCHOOL CAMPAIGN

Dr. Roberson has been heard to say again and again, "Follow divine direction." This is a must in all we do. One must pray about a theme, the proper time, the right leaders, special days, and every other area of the campaign.

The Pastor Must Take The Leadership

Every man of God ought to be a man of vision and compassion. He should have a goal to reach all people and a heart burdened to do the job. The pastor must stir the hearts of his people to do their best in this Sunday School campaign.

Meet With the Staff

The pastor should *plan* a time with the staff of the church (assistants, bus director, etc.) to discuss his primary *plans* for this campaign. A vision must be caught by each staff member and high goals set by each of these leaders.

Choose a Theme for the Campaign

This can express itself in a title — one that is broad enough to work with every part of the church and its outreach, yet specific enough to describe what you are attempting to do. Such titles as "Gospel Days Campaign," "Ten Thousand Campaign," "Every Heart Campaign," "Home and Family Campaign," "Faithfulness Campaign," "Fishing for Men Campaign," "Be One — Bring One Campaign," and a host of others have been used at our church. Perhaps the first time a Sunday School campaign is used it could simply be called "Our Three Greatest Months."

Include Every Organization of the Church

The Sunday School is potentially the greatest evangelistic arm of the church; so every other organization of the church (Training Union, mission groups, youth clubs, etc.) must work with the Sunday School, setting goals and attempting to reach the greatest heights ever in each area of the work of the church.

Decide on a Time

Many will want to run a three-month campaign in the fall and another three-month campaign in the spring. They will take the summer and winter a month at a time. Others may want to have a six-week campaign, while still others may choose another time period. Whatever the case, decide on a time.

Find Out What the Records Are

When the pastor states that he wants to reach an all-time high in every part of the church, this is what he must attempt to lead his people to do. Find out the highest Sunday School attendance, the biggest Training Union crowd, the most people who have ever been saved and baptized in a certain period, the highest offering, the largest amount given to missions, and the largest crowds to ever attend the preaching services. Determine to go over the top in each of these areas.

Name Special Days

It is a valuable thing to title each Sunday with a certain designation to set forth what is being attempted. It provides a "rallying point" for all. Notice the "natural days" that will fall within the given time period of the campaign (Christmas, Easter, church anniversary, pastor's anniversary, radio anniversary, etc.). Attempt to make these big days even bigger. In the

Banners in the main auditorium help to keep Sunday School goals and campaigns before the people.

planning sessions, one can simply list on somewhat of a work sheet the title for the campaign, the dates on which each Lord's Day falls, the natural big days; and then begin to give names to the other Sundays.

Put People to Work

Of course, the pastor and a few other key people are the ones most vitally involved in the campaign; but, at the same time, outstanding lay people can be placed in positions of leadership in this campaign. A certain individual can be placed over each month. One may want to go so far as to put a certain person over each Sunday. Whatever the case, put as many of your good people as possible to work. It would be a very good idea to put others of your people in lesser roles at this time in order to train them to help lead in the next Sunday School campaign.

Set Challenging Goals

Remember, you are attempting to go over the top of previous records. One may wish to set only one high attendance goal for the final Sunday, but this is not always the best. Individual class goals should be set to exceed anything the class has done in the past. Monthly and weekly attendance goals should also be set. If this method is used, it will help to break the big record on the final Sunday.

Commend the People for a Job Well Done

Many make the mistake of talking too much about those who have failed, when in reality nothing about failure needs to be said. Reward those who do make their goals. By doing this, one is actually encouraging those who have failed to do better.

Keep Your Motives Right

The Lord's people should be doing all they do because they love the Lord Jesus and want to build a work for His glory. It is not to be done to be seen of men or to make a name for oneself. Let us do it all for His eternal glory and based on the value of precious souls.

Here are some suggested themes for Sunday School campaigns during different months of the year.

JANUARY — Resolution Campaign, Genesis Campaign, 52 Club Campaign

FEBRUARY — Heart Campaign, Loyalty Campaign

MARCH — Marching to Sunday School Campaign

APRIL — New Life Campaign

MAY — Family Month (Baby Day, Mother's Day, Youth Day, Children's Day)

JUNE — Men For The Master (Father's Day)

JULY — Declaration of Dependence Campaign

AUGUST — Summer Jump Month

SEPTEMBER — Round-Up Month (rounding up all summer strays)

OCTOBER — Onward In October ("Onward Christian Soldiers")

NOVEMBER — Harvest Month

DECEMBER — His Month (emphasizing Christmas and His birth)

Use Great Songs and Bible Verses

In order to make the campaigns in Sunday School successful and to have the greatest impact, special songs and Bible verses should be used in conjunction with the campaign.

Examples —

Taxi Campaign — John 1:42 "And he brought him to Jesus . . ."

Faithfulness Campaign — Hebrews 10:25

Loyalty Campaign — Sing "Loyalty to Christ"

WORKSHEET FOR PLANNING A
SUNDAY SCHOOL CAMPAIGN

Title of the Campaign

_____

Time of the Campaign

_____

Name of Your Church

_____

Sunday Dates and Titles of Special Days

Sunday _____ Title _____

Plans for this day _____

_____

_____

_____

_____

Sunday _____ Title _____

Plans for this day _____

_____

_____

_____

_____

Sunday Dates and Titles of Special Days

Sunday _____ Title _____

Plans for this day _____

_____

_____

_____

_____

Sunday _____ Title _____

Plans for this day _____

_____

_____

_____

_____

Sunday _____ Title _____

Plans for this day _____

_____

_____

_____

_____

Purpose of the Campaign

_____

_____

_____

_____

Activities for Each Class

_____

_____

_____

_____

Special Choruses and Bible Verses to be Used

_____

_____

_____

_____

Awards to be Presented (If Used)

_____

_____

_____

_____

Notes for Ideas to Use in the Bus Ministry, Visitation Program, etc., As They Relate to the Sunday School Campaign:

CHAPTER

24

Put These Sunday School Campaigns to Use

*"Honor Christ and He will honor you and
your ministry."*

Two of the finest Sunday School campaigns in Highland Park
history were the "Big Kickoff" and "Gold Rush" campaigns.
Both were planned and designed by Dr. J. R. Faulkner and
were carried out in the exact form given here.

SUNDAY SCHOOL PROMOTION — Month of October, 1964

Highland Park Baptist Church, Chattanooga, Tennessee

Keep in mind that October is the first month in the new church
year at the Highland Park Baptist Church, so we used this to
emphasize our Sunday School campaign.

Motto:
"Go Forward"

Theme:
"The Big Kickoff " ("The Big Kickoff in '64 for Success in '65")

Purpose:
1. To reach and exceed in this October each Sunday's attendance of
   October a year ago.
2. To reach 100 new members for our Sunday School.
3. To encourage visitors — preferably those not belonging to or
   attending Sunday School at any other church.
4. To encourage attendance at the weekly Officers' and Teachers'
   Meeting and our weekly visitation program.

Plan:
A small football field scaled to eight feet in length was constructed
with every feature of a football field visible.

Each division of the Sunday School composed a team, with each
class and department in the division representing the individual

members. The Coach of each team was the superintendent of the division.

There being six divisions in our Sunday School, there were six wires run from one end of the field to the other. A small plastic or hard rubber football measuring about five inches in length was placed on each wire and painted in a distinct color to represent that team. Of course, all six colors were different.

As each team advanced, yardage was given instead of points; and the plan was for each team to receive as many touchdowns as possible within the month. Yardage was given as follows:

1 yard for each point above last year's attendance

5 yards for each new member

3 yards for each visitor

5 yards for reaching attendance goal for Officers' and Teachers' Meeting

1 additional yard could be given for each person from class who came out for the weekly visitation program.

Each Sunday was a special Sunday:

October 4	The Big Kickoff!
October 11	The Big Game Is On!
October 18	Carry That Ball!
October 25	Touchdown!

Special stationery was provided each week, giving emphasis to next Sunday's goal and slogan. Every class and department was urged to write letters to their members as well as to others whom they hoped to interest.

Awards:

A trophy was given to the superintendent of the department whose team won for the month.

A small trophy was given each week to the class making the most yardage in each division.

SUNDAY SCHOOL PROMOTION

Month of November, 1964

Theme: "GOLD RUSH '64"

This plan involved a wagon train leaving a particular point on the East Coast. We chose one city which we hoped to reach as we moved westward for each Sunday of the month.

The entire caravan was made up of six wagon trains, each train representing a department of the Sunday School, and each wagon in

"Gold Rush" Sunday School campaign.

the train representing a class or department within the division. A color was assigned to each of the trains. This was done by painting the top of the wagon used on our chart and writing in the name of the class or department represented.

For the chart, a long map was made indicating the route the caravan would take and showing the cities to be visited along the route. Small wagons of the old Conastoga type were cut out of index-weight cardboard and stuck with cellophane tape to the map to indicate their westward progress.

The superintendents in charge of each train were called "wagon masters," and the general superintendent who headed up the drive was called "trail boss" for the month.

The train stops chosen by us were:

November 1	Dodge City, Kansas
November 8	Silverton, Colorado
November 15	Cedar City, Utah
November 22	Carson City, Nevada
November 29	Sacramento, California

Mileage was given on the same basis as used in the October campaign for usual challenges given in any Sunday School campaign.

Awards:

For awards we wrote the mayors of these cities and asked them to send us a letter of welcome to the city, which was presented to the first wagon train to arrive or the wagon train having made the greatest progress during the week. We also made a key to the city, using plywood. This had "Welcome To Dodge City" on it, for instance. This was presented to the officers of the winning class.

We also asked the Chambers of Commerce in these various cities to send us curios, which were given to the leading wagons (classes or departments) in the winning train (division). All of this served to inspire everyone to work hard. No publicity was given as to what the curios would be.

As a final incentive, an old-fashioned washpot (not too large) was obtained, painted a shiny black, and filled with gold-wrapped candy. This was to represent the "pot of gold" to be given to the class or department (wagon) achieving the highest record for the month. This was given along with a letter of welcome to the city of Sacramento, California.

Churches using this idea should be careful to avoid contacting the same cities used by Highland Park. They might not be as willing to cooperate the second time.

We also add: Our Sunday School offered to pay for the curios from the different cities.

Other campaigns were as follows:

FISHERS OF MEN
Sunday School Campaign — Date
Name of Your Church

"Follow me, and I will make you fishers of men." Matthew 4:19

SPECIAL DAYS IN MAY

DATE — "Let's Go Fishing Sunday" Emphasis on soul winning and the Great Commission. Locate the Fish.

DATE — "Bait the Hook Sunday" Emphasis on the Bible and the message of the Gospel.

DATE — "Cast Sunday" Emphasis on the Visitation Program and places to go with the Gospel.

DATE — "Land Sunday" Emphasis on bringing someone to Sunday School that has been contacted during the month.

Special Chorus to be used

"I Will Make You Fishers of Men"

Decorations

Use fishing nets, boats, etc. for decorating rooms and the auditorium for the campaign.

THE VISITATION PROGRAM

Present a gold fish hook to all those who go visiting in the churchwide visitation.

Invitation cards like the following will be used by each class when inviting people to attend the class:

```
+--------------------------------------+
|        Our Sunday School Class       |
|        _____        |
|                                      |
|       Is Fishing for People — Date   |
|            (picture of fish)         |
|      Plan to Visit with Us This Sunday |
|            NAME OF CHURCH            |
|           Address of Church          |
+--------------------------------------+
```

Place these returning cards in a *fish bowl*. At the end of the month a card will be drawn from the bowl and a nice gift will be presented to the teacher of the class appearing on the card.

IN EACH SUNDAY SCHOOL CLASS
"Fatten The Fish"
50 lbs.

Start each class with a fifty-pound fish.

For each visitor attending the class during this campaign add 10 lbs. to the fish.

For each new member enrolled during the campaign add 20 lbs. to the class fish.

The class with the fattest fish at the end of the month proves they have done the best job.

APRIL IS "VICTORY" MONTH

Song: "V" Is For Victory!
Verse: I Corinthians 15:57

APRIL 5 – "VOLUNTEER" SUNDAY
"Victory Through Volunteers" For

1. Time
2. Tithe
3. Talents
4. Influence
5. Example
6. Energy

Volunteers for Jesus

APRIL 12 – *"VISION 'SUNDAY*
"Victory Through Renewed Vision"
1. Dedicated Living   4. Soul Winning
2. Bible Study   5. Second Coming of Christ
3. Prayer   6. Scripture Distribution

APRIL 19 – *"VISITATION SUNDAY*
"Victory Through Visitation"
1. Lost   4. House-to-House
2. Shut-In   **5. By Telephone**
3. Unchurched   6. By Mail

APRIL 26 – *VICTORY SUNDAY*
"Recapitulation Day"
1. Victory Parade   2. Victors Crowned

"Thine, O Lord, . . . Is The Victory"

I Chronicles 29:11

SONG:

"V" Is For Victory!

"V" is for victory!
Sing it out, 'tis a glorious word;
"V" is for victory,
It is ours through Christ our Lord.

Some days may be dark and drear;
In Christ the way's "all clear,"
For we have victory,
Victory in Christ our Lord.

VERSE:

"But thanks be to God, which giveth us the victory through our Lord Jesus Christ."

I Corinthians 15:57

I WILL BE ONE — I WILL BRING ONE
Sunday School Promotion
May 1977

The emphasis for the month will be on the Christian home —
REACHING HOMES FOR CHRIST

Special Days Will Include:

May 1— Men's Day	May 15 — Baby Day
May 8— Mother's Day	May 22 — Children's Day
	May 29 — Youth Day

"Baby Day."

Each week the group being recognized will seek to bring others with them to Sunday School (May 1 — Men bringing Men; May 8 — Women bringing Women; May 15 — Families with Babies bringing other Families with Babies; May 22 — Children bringing Children; May 29 — Young People bringing Young People). Everyone committing himself to "Be One and To Bring One."

We will be spotlighting the Sunday School classes and workers each week who teach the particular group recognized on Sunday (Men, Women, Babies, Children, Youth).

Teachers' and Officers' Meeting — A representative from each class will come forward each Wednesday night in the T and O Meeting when their name is called. If the goal has been reached, they will ring the bell, if not, they will sound the buzzer.

A personal testimony each Thursday night.

    April 28 ....Men
    May 5..Women
    May 12 ....Couple with Child
    May 19..Child
    May 26..Young Person

Each family of the church is encouraged to make a commitment to bring one family to visit with us at Highland Park Baptist Church in May. Our high attendance goal is 11,000 on May 29.

MYSTERY MONTH CAMPAIGN

Month of October good for this.
Use for whole church or
in Sunday School classes and departments.

1. *Mystery Speakers* — No one knows who the mystery speaker is until he stands to present his message.
2. *Mystery Piece of Mail* — Identify one piece of your mailing as such. The person receiving it must in turn bring it to church on Sunday for a special gift.
3. *Mystery Bulletin* — is labeled accordingly and is later recognized from the pulpit.
4. *Mystery Voices* — Play a short section of a tape or record, affording the group the opportunity to determine the voice.
5. *Mystery Character*
   a. Have folk dressed in biblical costumes to come to the platform; give three clues as to their identity. The persons accurately identifying the characters should be rewarded at the end of the month.
   b. Outstanding individuals in your church may be recognized and awarded bronze plaques.
6. Have entire congregation to search the Scriptures to find the word "mystery." Give a reward for the person finding it the most number of times.

SUNDAY SCHOOL BASEBALL

EACH CLASS WILL HAVE SIX BATTERS. THEY ARE:
1. CLASS VISITS
2. INVITED VISITORS
3. TEACHER VISITS
4. ATTENDING TEACHERS' MEETING
5. REACHING CLASS GOAL
6. GIVING TO BUILDING FUND

THEY WILL BAT IN THE ORDER ABOVE. THEY WILL BE SCORED AS FOLLOWS:
1. CLASS VISITS — DOUBLE
2. INVITED VISITORS — DOUBLE (A card bearing the name and class attended for each visitor must be placed in the folder where he or she is counted.)

3. TEACHER VISITS   1 — 2 = Single
                                  3 — 5 = Double
                                  6 — 9 = Triple
                    10 or more = Home Run

4. ATTENDING TEACHERS' MEETING = 1 Home Run

5. REACHING CLASS GOAL = 1 Home Run

The score will be determined by how many of the batters have scored after all have batted. If after all six have batted and there are no outs, an extra run will be added as a bonus.

BIG EXTRA BONUS
FOR EACH SOUL WON TO THE LORD = 5 HOME RUNS

The number of runs the department scores will be determined by adding the scores of all the classes in the department together and dividing by the number of classes. The answer will be half rounded. If the average is .5 or more, it will be rounded to the next whole number; if not, it will divert back to the whole number in the average. If a department reaches its goal, it will be awarded an extra run to be added to the score after the average is determined.

RUN = A SCORE AWARDED WHEN ALL FOUR BASES HAVE BEEN COVERED CONSECUTIVELY.
OUT = FAILURE OF BATTER TO REACH BASE.
SINGLE = BATTER REACHES FIRST BASE, ALL RUNNERS ADVANCE ONE BASE.
DOUBLE = BATTER REACHES SECOND BASE, ALL RUNNERS ADVANCE TWO BASES.
TRIPLE = BATTER REACHES THIRD BASE, ALL RUNNERS ADVANCE THREE BASES.
HOME RUN = BATTER ADVANCES ALL THE WAY AROUND THE BASES, BATTER AND ALL RUNNERS SCORE.
RUNNER = A BATTER BECOMES A RUNNER WHEN HE SAFELY REACHES 1st, 2nd, or 3rd BASE.

1. A trophy will be given to the teacher in each department with the most runs each Sunday.
2. A large trophy will be presented to the department superintendent that has the most runs at the end of the five weeks.

MULTIPLIED MIRACLES IN MAY CAMPAIGN 1962

This is the theme for the Sunday School campaign for the coming month. Dr. J.R. Faulkner is promotional leader.

SUNDAY, MAY 6, is SHERMAN ROBINSON DAY. We will be honoring the memory of Sherman Robinson who went to be with the

Lord one year ago. Chairmen for the day: Elgin Smith and Kenton Hixson. A picture of Mr. Robinson will be given to everyone in the adult classes.

SUNDAY, MAY 13, MOTHER'S DAY. There will be a gift for every lady present.

SUNDAY, MAY 20, ANNUAL BABY DAY. We are looking for more than 325 babies to be in the Cradle Roll Department. The Baby Day Parade will be held at 11:00 o'clock. See the beautiful babies in the beautifully decorated carriages. Gifts for all babies.

SUNDAY, MAY 27, BACCALAUREATE SUNDAY. Dr. David Allen will be the guest speaker for the evening service.

"LET FREEDOM RING CAMPAIGN 1961"

The July Sunday School campaign is under way. The two promotional superintendents, Mr. R.N. Land and Mr. John Miller, are working. We are all going to work with them. We want to make July a time of great victory. Please note the following announcements:

SUNDAY, JULY 9 — "FREEDOM OF SPEECH"

Encourage Sunday School members to witness to at least one person during the week.

SUNDAY, JULY 16 — "FREEDOM OF PRESS"

Sunday School workers will send out special letters emphasizing our freedom of the press. Give out tracts!

SUNDAY, JULY 23 — "FREEDOM OF ASSEMBLY"

Encourage prospects as well as members to assemble with us on this Lord's Day.

SUNDAY, JULY 30 — "FREEDOM FROM THE POWER OF SIN"

Encourage all members to give Christ the victory by their being in Sunday School and church on this last Sunday.

BRIEF IDEAS FOR SUNDAY SCHOOL CAMPAIGNS

March — Open Hand Month

March 1 — Open Hand to Visitors
March 8 — Open Hand to Members
March 15 — Open Hand to Unenlisted
March 22 — Open Hand to Students
March 29 — Open Hand to Everyone

Attendance Goal 3000

"Thou openest thine hand, and satisfiest the desire of every living thing."   *Psalm 145:16*

APPRECIATION MONTH

Teacher Appreciation Day
Superintendents Appreciation Day
Sunday School Workers Appreciation Day
Pastor Appreciation Day

SPOTLIGHT MONTH

On each Sunday of the month recognize a certain division of the Sunday School. Honor each worker.

Cradle Roll & Beginners Sunday
Primary & Junior Sunday
Intermediate & Youth Sunday
Adult & Special Classes Sunday

PERFECT SUMMER CAMPAIGN

Make this summer a perfect summer. Attend all church services every Sunday and every Wednesday prayer service!

"HEART'S DESIRE MONTH"

Scripture: Psalm 37:4

February is Enlistment Month:

THEME: ENLISTING HEARTS FOR CHRIST

GOAL 50 New Hearts

Sunday, February 2, Will Be

"BRING A HEART DAY"

(Bring a Heart — Get a Sweet Heart)

Awards To Classes Or Departments With Highest
Attendance — "Awards"
To Those With Lowest Attendance

10,000 CAMPAIGN

"Our Greatest Ever"

Together Let Us Do These (3) Things

I. Every Member of Highland Park Baptist Church determining to be a "Personal Invitation Committee" of one.
   a. Showing Compassion
   b. Showing Consistency
   c. Showing Christian Courtesy

II. Have the largest attendance in every ministry of our church in its history:

86

a. Enrolling at least one new person in every Sunday School Class each week. "Operation — Won by One"

b. On a given Sunday having over 10,000 people in Sunday School of our church breaking any attendance record of the past.

III. See more people saved and baptized during this three month period than in any other three months of our church history:

a. Much praying

b. Multitudes invited

THE SUNDAY SCHOOL TEACHER AND HIS CLASS INVOLVED IN "OPERATION — WON BY ONE"

This is such an important **Key** in our **10,000 Campaign.** The end result of teaching is to change the behavior of those who are being taught. In our case, it is attempting to produce Christ-likeness in the lives of every member of the Sunday School Class.

We are going to do something in each of our Sunday School Classes during our **"10,000 Campaign"** that will have an eternal effect upon the lives of people. It is called **"Operation — Won by One."** It is going to sound so simple — yet if done it will be **a profound achievement on the part of your Sunday School Class!**   Here it is:

We are asking that each Sunday School Class enroll one new person each week during our 10,000 Campaign. This means your class, not your department. The teacher with his own heart stirred will stir the people of his class to enroll one new person in their class each week. The teacher must lead the way — no one should get behind.

10 Outstanding Teachers:

At the end of our **"10,000 Campaign"** the 10 outstanding teachers of our Sunday School will have their names engraved on a beautiful plaque that will be displayed outside our Sunday School Office. The teachers whose names appear on this permanent plaque will be the names of those who do the best job motivating their class in the enrollment of new members. The top 10 teachers in new enrollment will be chosen.

IN OUTREACH

10,000 Doors Knocked On, 10,000 Personal Invitations Mailed, 10,000 Telephone Calls Made.

People from a certain area of our city recognized each week (a different area each week). Also to include surrounding communities.

A beautiful gift will be given to each person who has brought 10 or more people to our church during our 10,000 Campaign.

25

Make Use of Special Days

"If we do not begin in prayer, we shall end in failure."

The subject of special days in the lives of God's people is nothing new. Through all the Bible we read of the celebration of special days. In the Old Testament we find such special days and occasions as the Passover, Pentecost, and Tabernacles. In the New Testament we witness again the celebration of special days. It is evident that the Lord Jesus, His disciples, and His apostles after Him used these special days to an advantage in getting the gospel message to lost multitudes.

Marion Lawrence, noted Sunday School authority of the past, stated:

> "Mention is made of special days in Bible times for the purpose of showing that they had an important place in the program of the development of God's people. They served to emphasize certain great truths and, at the same time, to create a spirit of loyalty and enthusiasm that went far towards driving away discouragement and sustaining with fervor their religious and national life."

The use of special days can serve the same purpose in the church today. The interest and excitement of the people can be stirred to express a greater loyalty to Christ and what He has called us to do.

It goes without saying that there are obstacles to overcome in the use of special days in Sunday School; but if special days honor Christ and help to get lost sinners under the sound of the Gospel, then let's get busy and plan a "Special Day" in Sunday School.

HERE'S WHY WE HAVE SPECIAL DAYS

Special Days Help to Place Emphasis on Soul Winning

Everything we do in the local New Testament church should be done as a move toward reaching lost souls. Every recommendation coming before our people should be a recommendation based on the value of precious souls. The end result of every financial expense should be to tell someone of Christ and His power to save. Special days are a great asset in letting everyone know that our aim is to reach the unsaved with the message of the Gospel. The end result of every special day is to get folks saved.

Special Days Increase Our Vision
And Add an Air of Excitement

Many churches across our country have lost their spirit of adventure and conquest. All of us need a frontier to conquer. There lives within most of us a desire for adventure and challenge. To set high goals on special days and to work toward reaching certain goals helps us to see greater possibilities and enlarge our vision. All this creates an air of excitement and expectancy among the people.

There Are Certain Natural Days on the Calendar
That We Need to Take Advantage Of

Days such as Christmas, Easter, Mother's Day, Valentine's Day, New Year's Day, The Fourth of July, and Thanksgiving Day are already very special days in the hearts of many people. We can use this to get greater crowds under the sound of the Gospel.

Special Days Add Variety
To the Total Program of the Church

The old expression, "Variety is the spice of life" seems to fit well here. Of course, we realize that certain things never change; but at the same time, to maintain a high interest among our people in the work, we must stay out of the "rut." Business people, companies, and sales personnel realize the necessity of change and variety; and those of us in the work of the Lord need to see the advantage of this also. There will be no change in our plan to give out the Word of God each week, but we must add variety to our program. One excellent way to do this is through special days.

Dr. Charles Weigle singing. Special days can be used to honor the life and ministry of faithful servants of the Lord.

Special Days Help to Increase Our Attendance

Each Sunday School should seek to enlarge its attendance. Numbers represent people, and reaching people with the Gospel is our business. If we want to see people saved and converts following Christ in baptism week after week, then we must have new people in our Sunday School classes each Sunday.

> *So the servant came, and shewed his lord these things. Then the master of the house being angry said to his servant, Go out quickly into the streets and lanes of the city, and bring in hither the poor, and the maimed, and the halt, and the blind. And the servant said, Lord, it is done as thou hast commanded, and yet there is room. And the lord said unto the servant, Go out into the highways and hedges, and compel them to come in, that my house may be filled.*
> *Luke 14:21-23*

The Lord Jesus wants His house filled. Let us seek to fill it for His glory.

**Special Days Provide a Goal to Work Toward
And Unify the Efforts of Our People
In a Common Purpose**

Every organization, as well as every individual, should be involved in the special day. In the planning stage at the very beginning, let the people know that this is something we all must work toward. Someone has said, "If you want people with you on the landing, make sure they are with you on the take-off." A local church is a fellowship of baptized believers, voluntarily uniting themselves together to worship the Lord and carry out the great commission of the Lord Jesus. The church can work together in the special day.

**Special Days Allow Many People to Be Put to Work
And Special Talents to Be Used**

It is one thing to win people to Christ but quite another to work with them, seeking to see them grow in the Lord. The Christian must be serving the Lord in order to grow. Special days allow many people to work and create a demand for art work, children's ministries, and many other areas where people can develop in their service to the Saviour.

SOME THINGS TO AVOID
WHEN CONSIDERING SPECIAL DAYS

When considering special days for your Sunday School, there are certain things we must avoid.

Being Sidetracked by a Few Complainers

Satan does not like any soul-winning emphasis. Be sure that if your special day is planned to reach the lost, there will be some type of opposition. The test of our sincerity in serving God is not in what it takes to get us started; it is in what it takes to stop us after we start in our service to the Lord. Be sure the people are informed about what is going on, and do not allow a handful of pessimistic people to kill the program.

Violation of Biblical Principles

Some have been heard to say, "We will do anything for a crowd." This is a dangerous philosophy. Do not make the mistake of having some supercolossal day that results in great harm to the church because it "smacked too much of this world." One often-heard complaint of special days is that they are sometimes not compatible with the dignity and spirituality of the Gospel. In some places, this complaint may be valid; but it can be avoided. Every special guest speaker must be a genuine born-again Christian if we expect the blessing of God upon our work.

Thinking Promotion Is All We Need

The building of a great Sunday School must combine reaching lost souls with teaching the Word of God. We can get lots of folks to attend with special promotion, but we must have a sound Bible-based program if we expect to keep them. *The greatest asset to any Sunday School is the uninterrupted teaching of the Word of God Sunday after Sunday.*

HINTS ON HOW TO HAVE A SPECIAL DAY IN SUNDAY SCHOOL

Follow the Leadership of the Holy Spirit

No one is more concerned about the salvation of lost souls than our Lord. Let us be led of God in having any special day. Divine direction is an absolute must.

Pray for the Blessing of God upon the Work

All our ideas, our plans, and promotions should be Christ-honoring and should glorify God. Let us praise God for every goal reached and every soul saved. God will bless that kind of effort. Nothing should ever be attempted if we cannot ask God to bless it.

Be Excited and Enthusiastic

Very little is ever accomplished without enthusiasm. Sometimes ideas are more "caught" than taught. People need to see a leader that is excited, one that possesses a determined enthusiasm with purpose.

Plan Ahead

The thinking person realizes the value of planning ahead. Success does not just happen. Think the thing through. Get all your ideas together. Look at the calendar. "Those who fail to plan — plan to fail."

Get People Involved

Have as many people sold on the idea as possible from the very beginning. Glean ideas from your people. At Highland Park we have had hundreds of people turn in suggestions for special days. In order for people to put their best foot forward in the program, we must endeavor to make them a part of it.

Start Promoting Early

The failure of many big ideas is in the fact that we never took the proper amount of time to inform our people. There could be a problem in starting so early that we tire people before the event even takes place, but most of us will never be guilty of this error. Allow plenty of time to saturate and inform the people of the special day.

Begin the Promotion Right

We only have one opportunity to make a good first impression. People remember first things — how it was spoken — the way in which it was spoken. Make those first announcements concerning your special day in such a way that will arouse the interest of people.

Set Your Goals High

People must be challenged. If a Sunday School is running 65 in average attendance, people will work harder and get more enthused about reaching 100 than they will about reaching 80. At times it is helpful to let classes set their own goals. This way they may feel more of a responsibility in reaching it. The goal should be set high enough so that the people know everyone must work together in order to reach it.

Decide on Methods

The imagination must be stirred, and people must be challenged. Motivation should be our concern. Methods must be chosen that will motivate. Of course, the highest motive for service is love for the Lord Jesus. There are a number of things that can be done. Perhaps sign-up campaigns can be used. Get everyone to pledge to be present. Captains can be selected to enlist a certain number to be present on the special day. Many times competition between classes or organizations in the church can arouse people to work. Simply find the best methods and use them.

Get Folks to Bring Friends

Everyone knows someone they can bring to Sunday School. Our task is to motivate them with God's help to go after that particular person and bring them in. It may be a friend, a family member, a business associate, or a neighbor. There is someone they can bring.

Use Each Organization

The one organization in the church with the most potential is the Sunday School. In preparing for the special day, every organization needs to be busy — deacons, trustees, women's groups, youth fellowship, and any other organizations need to work toward reaching the goal on the special day.

Stir Up the Children

Boys and girls know so many people that they could bring to Sunday School. They are acquainted with many friends who need to be saved. Perhaps the girl and boy who bring the most visitors can be crowned the king and queen among the children. Never underestimate the ability of children to bring others to Sunday School.

Make Much of the Mail

Send out invitations. Write all the membership. Make a personal list of prospects, and send them a letter. Encourage your people to write their friends. Provide postcards for church members to send to others. Get the word out to as many people as possible.

Work at It with All Your Heart

Hard work is an absolute must. There is no magic formula. We must roll up our sleeves and get busy.

CHAPTER

26

A Special Sunday For Every Sunday of the Year

"We have one opportunity to make a good first impression."

The following list of special days is given with hope of being a means of stirring the thinking of Sunday School leaders, pastors, and superintendents alike. These days are simply a way of adding interest in Sunday School attendance. When people come under the influence of the Word of God in a Bible teaching Sunday School, the Lord is going to speak to their hearts, and lives will be changed.

ATHLETE SUNDAY

People of all ages are interested in athletics. Some churches have even had a "super bowl" contest in their Sunday Schools with one division against another serving as teams in the bowl game. Whatever the methods used, an all out attempt should be made to reach every athlete in the area with the Gospel. Invite all the high school athletes and their coaches to be special guests of the Sunday School. A Christian coach can be called on to give a testimony in the worship service. Many interesting and unusual things can be done.

ANNIVERSARY SUNDAY

There are many anniversaries that could be celebrated on an Anniversary Sunday. One might be the founding of the church. Another could be the date of the pastor's coming to the church. Honor the pastor on this day. Express your appreciation for his faithful ministry.

BACK-TO-SCHOOL SUNDAY

Back-to-School Sunday can be quite a day for your church. All those who have gone back to school receive a special invita-

95

tion to be present Sunday. Each Sunday School class that teaches school age children must set special goals for this day. Each school student will receive a gift that can be used in school. All school faculty and teachers will receive recognition.

BIBLE SUNDAY

The Bible is the book of the Sunday School. Everyone should bring their Bible to Sunday School. Every teacher should teach from the Bible. Inform people on the right translation of the Bible to use. Give them a daily plan for reading the Bible through each year. Present a new Bible to all those who read it through.

BIRTHDAY SUNDAY

Everyone loves a birthday. Plan a big Birthday Sunday for the pastor. Invite everyone to the party. Use party invitations. Not only children but adults also will enjoy this. Make this an unusual party. The pastor can give gifts to all present instead of those present bringing gifts. The "birthday award" will be given by the pastor to the one bringing the most people to the party. Present the pastor with a beautiful cake and sing "Happy Birthday" to him in the service.

BOOM SUNDAY

This is a great idea to bring people to Sunday School. BOOM stands for — Bring One Or More. BOOM tags should be provided for each person bringing one or more to Sunday School.

BREAK-THE-RECORD SUNDAY

Have every Sunday School class and teacher set a goal to break the record in their class. Work on it from a class level. Find out the highest attendance in each class, and recognize the teachers whose classes break the record.

CHILDREN'S DAY

Attempt to get as many children as possible under the sound of the Gospel on one Sunday. Conduct children's services throughout the week in every area of the city (neighborhoods, apartment buildings, etc.). Set goals for every children's class and department. Provide a special guest in every children's department of our Sunday School (magicians, costumed Bible characters, clowns, etc.). All will give out the gospel message. Special awards should be given to every child bringing a friend to Sunday School. Decorations in every Sunday School assembly room. Give a very special award to the department director who has the greatest number of visitors present and to the director enrolling the greatest number of new people in Sunday School. Crown a children's king and queen in each class. The boy and girl who bring the most visitors would receive the crown.

C.F. — CAR FULL SUNDAY

Plan a C.F. Sunday. Mention the two letters C.F. four or five weeks before you observe the special C.F. Sunday. Everyone will begin to wonder what C.F. stands for. Many questions will be asked. Posters with the two letters along with the date for the C.F. Sunday need to be placed on the walls of the Sunday School. Announce one week before the special day what C.F. stands for, and encourage every member to bring his car full to Sunday School.

CHRISTMAS SUNDAY

Give Christmas presents to all the children. Make telephone calls to hundreds of people in your city, inviting them to enjoy Christmas Sunday with you.

CITY-COUNTY HELPERS SUNDAY

We must teach people respect for those in positions of authority, and at the same time seek to win to Christ those who are in positions of authority. This special day is designed for the express purpose of building good will in the city, teaching respect for authority, and winning the lost. Every city official should be sent a personal invitation to be present in the service. Prepare a list of those who plan to be in attendance. Fire trucks, police cars, ambulances, and other vehicles should be on display for the children. A number of Christian officials may give their testimonies in Sunday School classes.

COMPEL SUNDAY

Again and again we must stress the importance of going after people with the gospel message. Sometimes it is easy for Sunday School classes and departments to let up on their soul-winning emphasis. Compel Sunday means just what it says. Go out and compel the people to come in. Have each class prepare a list of prospects for their class to compel to come. Plan to visit each of these prospects and compel them to be in the class the following Sunday.

DAY OF REJOICING

Luke 2:20 tells us that after the shepherds had seen the Lord, they were rejoicing. This day works well for the Sunday after Christmas. Invite some special guest with an outstanding testimony to be present. Perhaps this can be someone who has had hardships but still rejoices. The shepherds left the manger rejoicing. Let us place great emphasis on the day of salvation in the life of every believer present in the service. It will be their own personal day of rejoicing.

DEACONS' SUNDAY

People of the church need to know who the deacons are and what they do. This is a real opportunity for a pastor to encourage and exhort his men. Recognize each deacon and his family. Ask the chairman and perhaps one other to give their personal testimonies of how they got saved.

DEDICATION SUNDAY

This special day in Sunday School may be observed in connection with the opening of a new building, the beginning of a revival meeting, or just to call attention to the importance of having a dedicated Christian life. The need for dedication can never receive too much emphasis. Call attention to the things that should characterize the dedicated child of God. Challenge each Sunday School teacher and pupil to a greater degree of dedication to Christ.

DETERMINATION SUNDAY

This world is filled with quitters. Many of them are professing Christians. A special day in Sunday School should be set aside to honor those who have "stayed with it" — the kind who just will not quit. There are many wonderful people in every local church who have been through many trials but have been people of determination and great faith in God. Emphasize the importance of faithfully serving the Lord and never wavering. These people influence others greatly.

DOUBLE DAY

Double day is a day set aside to recognize all the twins in our city. Everyone will invite all the twins they know to the Sunday School. Also each member is asked to bring someone to be his double.

EXCEL-IN-FAITHFULNESS SUNDAY

The best thing that can be said about a Christian is that he is faithful. Every Christian should strive to excel in faithfulness. Be faithful in church attendance. Attend each of the stated services of the church. Be faithful in Bible study. Do not miss a single Sunday in Sunday School. Set a goal to read the Bible through at least once each year. Be faithful in prayer. Spend a certain portion of each day talking to God. Pray for others. Be faithful in soul winning. The lost will never hear of Christ if we do not go after them with the message of the Gospel.

FAMILY SUNDAY

Family days need to be planned in the Sunday School to encourage all members of the family to be faithful to God and win lost families to Christ. Setting aside a day called Family Day gives people an opportunity and an open door to reach their lost family members for Christ. Many say that talking to their own loved ones is the most difficult task they have. Recognize every complete family present. Pictures may even be taken of these families. At least one week before Family Day, members should turn in names of lost loved ones that they are attempting to get to church.

FRIEND SUNDAY

Friend Day can be the biggest day of the year in your church. The principle is simple — "Everyone brings a friend to Sunday School." Cards stating, "I will be one — I will bring one" are signed by each member. Use a little chorus to promote attendance — "I will be one, I will bring one in Sunday School Sunday." (Sing twice to the tune of the chorus in "Love Lifted Me") Encourage each class to double its attendance.

GENESIS SUNDAY

Of course, the name Genesis implies beginning. This is a perfect Sunday for the first Lord's Day of the new year. Every member is encouraged to start the new year right by being in church and attending every service the first Sunday of the new year. An extra added emphasis on this day can be the suggestion that everyone join the "52 CLUB" for the new year. The following card may be used.

Unless providentially hindered, I will be faithful in attending Sunday School each of the fifty-two Sundays this year.

NAME _____

ADDRESS _____

CLASS _____

GRANDPARENTS' SUNDAY

This is a very simple idea to invite grandparents to Sunday School. Grandparents of church members will be recognized. Lost loved ones who are grandparents will be brought to Sunday School. Through the visitation program, all grandparents will be invited to be special guests.

GRATEFUL SUNDAY

A thankful heart is a necessary part of the Christian life. On "Grateful Sunday," each person present will be encouraged to count his blessings. Special emphasis will be placed on recalling the day of one's salvation. The grateful person seeks to help others, so each person bringing a visitor will receive a grateful award.

GUEST SUNDAY

Guest Sunday should be a great day. Every visitor in our church is our honored guest. Each member will be asked to turn in the name of a guest he or she plans to bring on Guest Sunday. Beautiful gifts will be presented to each guest present.

HAPPY BIRTHDAY AMERICA SUNDAY

Patriotism among many Americans is a thing of the past. How desperately we need good old "red-blooded," "flag-waving" Americans today. Happy Birthday America Sunday should be observed on the Sunday before the 4th of July. Urge every child of God to declare his loyalty to America by being present on this Sunday. Sing patriotic songs, honor all branches of the service, and pray for national leaders. Government officials may also be invited as special guests.

HARVEST SUNDAY

Harvest Sunday may be celebrated during the fall of the year. Each class should attempt to have its biggest harvest ever on this Sunday (largest number present). One pastor ingeniously named each of his Sunday School classes after something grown in the garden (beets, greenbeans, peas, corn, potatoes, etc.) and asked who could produce the largest crop from the seed with which they began (those already attending).

HOMEGOING SUNDAY

This special day will cause people to think about eternity, seek to get the lost saved, and stir the heart of every Christian to serve the Lord more faithfully. There is an eternal home in heaven for the Christian. Though loved ones are in heaven, what they have done for Christ lives on to bless our lives. Special emphasis should be placed on heaven; sing songs about heaven; and emphasize the fact that there is singing in heaven. Possibly mention a number of people who held offices in the church who are now in heaven. A special invitation should be sent to all those in your area who have lost loved ones in the past year to attend the service. Present them with a lovely gift. A beautiful song about heaven could be used to open the service. A number of Sunday School classes could set special goals in honor of someone who had been a member, or even a teacher in their class, but who is now in heaven.

INVENTORY SUNDAY

Businesses take inventory, and so should individual Christians and churches. Inventory Sunday should be conducted to find out what has been accomplished in each class and organization of the church. Special goals will be given to each

Sunday School class. Awards will be given to those going over the top. Recognition should be given to each class that has done an outstanding job.

LADIES AND GENTLEMEN SUNDAY

Everyone loves the right kind of competition. This special Sunday we will have the ladies competing against the men for the highest attendance on this Sunday. Each side will be led by a capable team. In some churches, it would be good for the men to meet in one room and the ladies in another for Sunday School. A special speaker may be invited for each large class. The men will, of course, be encouraged to bring men and the women to bring women. This Sunday, properly planned and promoted, will cause many lost adults to be under the sound of the Gospel.

LETTER SUNDAY

This is such a simple idea but one that works very well. Most people love to receive things in the mail. Each Sunday School class should faithfully mail a class letter to each member every week. "Letter Sunday" places emphasis on the importance of this contact. Have a special Sunday School letterhead printed for this mailing. Perhaps a suitable one can be purchased from a printing company that specializes in "attention-getting" letterheads for businesses. Send the letter out to each member and each prospect with a good message about the Sunday School inside.

LOYALTY SUNDAY

Every Christian should be loyal. Loyalty to Christ and His church is a must. Every member will be urged to achieve new heights in loyalty not only in attendance but in soul winning, going, praying, Bible reading, and every other area of his Christian life.

MAY DAY

This special day may be observed on any Sunday in the month of May or especially on the first Sunday in May. The emphasis is on "Christian alert." Be prepared in this troubled world to put forth an all out effort for Christ. The Bible has a great deal to say about preparation. Let each Sunday School class work on this idea and send the "May Day" alert to each of their members to be present for Sunday School.

Dr. J. R. Faulkner leading the inspiring song service of the Highland Park Baptist Church.

MEDICAL SUNDAY

Send personal invitations to doctors of the city to attend. Have each member invite his personal physician. Seek to have a specialist from each field (head, heart, feet, etc.). Also invite all other medical personnel (including hospital staff). Have special places for hospital volunteer organizations to sit. Give special gifts to all those who have been patients in the hospitals during the past year. Use the song, "The Great Physician." Have a nursing ensemble sing a special number. Invite all those preparing for the medical field, pre-med and schools of nursing to be present for the service. Have some dedicated Christian doctor of the city to give his testimony.

MUSICAL SUNDAY

Place emphasis on the importance of music in worship. Skits could be given during Sunday School assemblies on the birth of about five or ten hymns or the life of a great hymnwriter, (Fanny Crosby, for example). All musicians of the city should be invited. Reveal to your people the ten favorite songs of your church. Each member could vote for three songs the week before. Recognize the work of those in the musical program. Special invitations should go out to all music lovers.

MYSTERY SUNDAY

In the work of Sunday School promotion and special days, if the imagination of people can be stirred, a victory can be accomplished. On "Mystery Sunday," the curiosity of the entire Sunday School should be aroused. Announce that there will be a mystery speaker in the Sunday School. Give clues to the identity of the speaker. Change the usual program around to make it somewhat mysterious. Use your imagination.

NEIGHBOR DAY

A great emphasis should be placed on bringing our neighbors to church. Every visitor is an honored guest. A lovely book on salvation and serving God can be presented to each person who brings his or her neighbor. The book would be given to the neighbor.

NO ABSENT "T" SUNDAY

Every Sunday School teacher will be challenged to work

toward having no absentees in his class. The following letter should be sent to every class member.

Dear _____ ,

More xhan ever we wanx you xo be presenx xhis Sunday for Sunday School ax xhe Highland Park Bapxisx Church. In recenx days some of our regular axxenders have been ill, so we have had absenxees from xhe Sunday School. Please help us go over xhe xop wixh a record-breaking axxendance.

By xhe way, I guess by now you are wondering why we have lefx oux all xhe "T's" in xhis lexxer. THE REASON IS THAT WE HAVE BEEN HAVING SOME ABSENT "T's" LATELY, AND WE JUST DON'T HAVE ENOUGH TO USE IN THIS LETTER. The only one left to go around is enclosed in this letter. So please come this Sunday and bring the enclosed "T."

Signed: S.S. Superintendent
Pastor

Enclose in the letter a letter (T) on a sheet of paper to return.

PICTURE SUNDAY

Announce to your people, "One of our finest and most interesting days in the Sunday School will be on next Sunday! At this time, pictures will be made of all classes and departments. Be sure to be present so that your picture can be included with your class. Reprints will be available at a later time." All pictures must be made between 9:45 and 10:00 a.m. Each teacher must ask that every pupil be present for this picture-taking.

P. I. — PERSONAL INVITATION SUNDAY

No invitation is quite as powerful as a personal invitation. Set a goal to give out so many personal invitations the week before "P. I. Sunday." Print a nice folder about the Sunday School. Assign each class to a certain area of the city to personally invite people to Sunday School. Instruct the people to take the name and address of each interested prospect. Each class will have a goal to extend so many personal invitations.

PRESIDENT SUNDAY

One Sunday of the year should be set aside as President Sunday. The main emphasis of the day would be to remind people of their duty to pray for the President of the United States. If a letter is sent early enough to the President explaining the purpose of this day, he will send a letter back (if requested) expressing his gratitude. This letter may be copied and a copy given to each person present. Also the presidents of companies, school classes, organizations, and anyone else having the title of president should be invited to the Sunday School and should receive special recognition.

RELATIVES SUNDAY

Many times the providing of an open door to witness to relatives proves to be all that is necessary to win them to Christ. This day is designed to reach loved ones. Send letters to all class members' relatives, urging them to be present. Call every nonmember relative and member relative to urge them to be in Sunday School and church. Encourage each church family to personally visit their relatives and bring them to Sunday School.

ROUND TO-IT SUNDAY

Many novelty shops have sold small, round wooden coins with "Round To-It" imprinted on them. Many people state they will come to Sunday School when they get around to it. Well, announce to everyone that you are going to have "Round To-It" Sunday. Everyone in Sunday School will receive an official Round "To-It" as they have gotten around to coming to Sunday School.

ROUND-UP SUNDAY

Round-Up Sunday is usually held just after the close of summer. It is an attempt to round up all the "strays" plus every new person possible for the Sunday School. A western theme can be carried out through the entire day. Each class has a goal to "rope" so many for Round-Up Day. Children love this cowboy emphasis, and it can prove an exciting day for all.

SECOND COMING SUNDAY

We celebrate Christ's birth as a babe in the manger and His resurrection from the grave. Why not celebrate the fact of His coming again. This is not an attempt to set a date for His return, but it is a time to place emphasis on the fact that He is coming again. Ask the question, "Where would you be Sunday

Choir of the 1890's singing on "Round-Up Day."

if you knew Christ was coming again Sunday?" He could return. Sing songs of His return. Set Sunday School goals in each class that would please Him. Emphasize the need to get our hearts right to meet Him. Award a book on the return of Christ to each visitor present.

SENIOR SUNDAY

On the Sunday closest to school graduation, have Senior Sunday in your church. Send invitations to every institution in the city that plans to graduate students. The graduates will be your special guests for this Sunday. Gifts will be presented to each graduate present.

SIGN-UP SUNDAY

One of the most successful Sunday School ideas is the idea of a sign-up campaign. Many churches have reported great successes using this method. Often invitations are extended to Sunday School prospects without getting any definite commitment from the prospect to attend the class. Each class member should make an agreement to sign up a certain number of people to attend on Sign Up Sunday. Goals are set not for attendance in the class but rather for the number of people signed up. You can expect around fifty percent of those who were signed up to attend in most cases.

SOMEDAY SUNDAY

So many people are heard to say, "Someday I plan to come." Make a great announcement. SOMEDAY IS FINALLY HERE!

Set the date for Someday Sunday. This day is to encourage every "excuse maker" to be in Sunday School. This emphasis should also be extended to certain areas of the Christian life where people tend to make excuses about starting someday (visitation, Bible reading, etc.).

START RIGHT SUNDAY

All of us need a time of "new beginnings." Many people think of this at the start of a new year. Perhaps it would be the beginning of the calendar year or the start of a new Sunday School teaching year (usually Oct. 1). This is a good time to have Start Right Sunday. Begin the new year right by doing everything you planned to do for Christ in the old year but did not. Attend Sunday School on the very important "first Sunday" — start right!

A-TASTE-OF-HEAVEN SUNDAY OR HEAVENLY SUNDAY

Place the emphasis on heaven. Use only the songs about heaven in the worship service. Extend special invitations to all those in your area who have lost loved ones in the past year to attend the services. Get a letter to them. Some book or booklet on heaven should be given to everyone bringing a visitor (perhaps Dr. Rice's little book on heaven).

TAXI SUNDAY

Our automobiles should be used as TAXIS for the Lord. Invite others to Sunday School; and offer to go by, pick them up, and *bring them* on Sunday. Have a certain number of "taxis" operating on this Sunday, bringing people to Sunday School so that they can hear the Gospel. Use every means at your command: telephone, letters, personal contacts, and especially your automobile to get people to Sunday School. Set a new record on TAXI SUNDAY.

TEACHER SUNDAY

Recognize all the faculty and teachers in area schools. Show your appreciation to your Sunday School teachers. Honor all your retired teachers present in the service. Recognize the teacher who has taught school for the longest period of time. Recognize the Sunday School teacher who has taught Sunday School for the greatest number of years.

TEAM AND COACH DAY

Send a personal letter to the athletic department of every school in your area, requesting the presence of the team and coach for Team and Coach Sunday at your church. A special well-known Christian athlete could be present to give his testimony in the service. A section will be reserved for each of those teams planning to be present. The name of the school in their school colors will appear on the pew.

TELEPHONE SUNDAY

The following is a sample conversation to be used in inviting others to Sunday School on Telephone Sunday. Conversation: "Hello, John? Say, next Sunday is TELEPHONE Sunday at our church, and I just called to invite you to visit with us Sunday." Take the time to pick up your phone and invite at least *FIVE* of your friends to Sunday School. Push *TELEPHONE SUNDAY!* Give God enough of your time to make at least five phone calls. Everyone can get involved.

TOPPLE-THE-TOP SUNDAY

Every class and department will be given specific goals for Sunday School. The goal will be their highest attendance plus one. Topple the top! Beautiful Bible and New Testament, autographed by men in top positions in our nation, can be presented to those who bring the largest number of visitors.

TRANSPORTATION SUNDAY

This big day will attract lots of attention. Ask your people to use every available means to come to church this Sunday. Awards should be given to the five most unique modes of transportation. Announce Operation — "Auto-mo-fill." Everyone must seek to fill his automobile with people on that Sunday. Pack the car with people.

V.I.P. SUNDAY

Everyone likes to feel important. We must seek to let people know that they are important to God and to God's people. Print V.I.P. cards, and hand them out to people inviting them to be with us on V.I.P. Sunday. Every visitor in our church is a V.I.P. — very important person.

VISITOR-PER-PEW SUNDAY

New people in the services usually means that many will be saved. On this special day, each pew in the building should

"Transportation Sunday", Mr. Elgin Smith and Dr. Lee Rober-son.

be assigned to a certain team of people. This team is charged with having a first time visitor sitting on that pew on Visitor-Per-Pew Sunday.

WON-BY-ONE SUNDAY

The Lord Jesus has commanded us to go into all the world and preach the Gospel to every creature. Evangelizing the lost one by one is something every Christian should be engaged in. Challenge every Christian in the church to win one to Christ and bring that one to church. Won by One Sunday would be a day to recognize soul winners and those they have won to Christ. With this special day you may begin an enrollment campaign. Ask each Sunday School class to enroll one new person each week during the campaign. This means the class, not the department. The teacher with his own heart stirred will stir the people of his class to enroll one new person in his class each week. The teacher must lead the way — no one should get behind. At the end of the campaign, the ten outstanding teachers of the Sunday School will have their names engraved on a beautiful plaque that will be displayed outside the Sunday School Office. The teachers whose names appear on this per-manent plaque will be the names of those who do the best job motivating their class in the enrollment of new members. The top ten teachers in new enrollment will be chosen.

27

Scores of Special Days To Meet Special Needs

"The Sunday School is the greatest evangelistic arm of the church."

There are many special needs that arise in the work of the Lord. From time to time, different areas of the ministry need special emphasis. Special days in Sunday School help to place this emphasis where it is needed.

HONOR OUTSTANDING PEOPLE

There are times when certain personalities need to be recognized. They may be people who are known only by the church, or they may even be somewhat famous.

PASTOR'S DAY

MAYOR'S SUNDAY

Invite your mayor and mayors of surrounding cities as special guests.

VIP SUNDAY

HYLES SUNDAY

DEACONS' SUNDAY

Introduce deacons, and their families to the church. Take a picture of the entire group.

DR. JACK VAN IMPE SUNDAY

GARTENHAUS SUNDAY

PARKER SUNDAY

WORKERS' APPRECIATION DAY

Recognize and present gifts to all workers.

FAULKNER SUNDAY

WEIGLE SUNDAY

KIM WICKES SUNDAY

KING AND QUEEN FOR A DAY

Elect a king and queen from the Sunday School.

WASHINGTON'S BIRTHDAY

Recognize the lives of great Americans on this day.

FAMOUS FOLKS SUNDAY

Recognize outstanding people in the church on this day.

GOVERNOR'S DAY

The state governor should be the special guest.

MR. AND MISS/MRS. SUNDAY SCHOOL SUNDAY

RICE DAY

STRESS RESPONSIBILITIES

Church members need to be reminded of certain responsibilities from time to time. Special days may serve this purpose.

INVENTORY SUNDAY

GRATEFUL SUNDAY

Turn in notes with blessings written on them.

TRANSPORTATION SUNDAY

PRAYER DAY OR ALTAR SUNDAY

Recognize the importance of prayer.

OPEN BIBLE SUNDAY

This name could be given to the first Sunday
of the Bible Conference.

COMBAT SUNDAY

We are in a fight against the world,
the flesh, and the devil.

POST OFFICE SUNDAY

Use the mail in the Lord's work.

RAINBOW SUNDAY

Get promises from people to attend Sunday School.

WELCOME SUNDAY

ANSWER SUNDAY
Christ is the answer.
HONOR EMPLOYER SUNDAY
Every employee invite his or her employer.
MAIL SUNDAY
TAXI SUNDAY
Use each car for a TAXI to
fill with people for Sunday School.
GO FOR GOALS SUNDAY
LETTER SUNDAY
Place another emphasis on using the mail.
TELEPHONE SUNDAY
Encourage the use of the phone to reach others.
BE ONE OF THE BUNCH SUNDAY
Each class is a banana tree. Each one present counts as one of
the bunch.
FILL YOUR CAPSULE SUNDAY
Each car is a capsule.
TRY HARDER SUNDAY
Have more than the Sunday before.
VITAMIN B1 SUNDAY
Everyone receives and returns a vitamin B1.
DARE TO DO
YOUR BEST FOR THE LORD SUNDAY
FULL ATTENDANCE SUNDAY
GO TO CHURCH DAY
BOOK DAY
INSPECTION DAY
STANDARDS DAY
POST CARD DAY
NEW TESTAMENT DAY
VISITING DAY (SUNDAY AFTERNOON)
ON TIME DAY

Kenton Hixson, Highland Park Sunday School Superintendent for over 15 years, and M. J. Parker, Bus Director for over 25 years.

PERSONAL CONTACT SUNDAY

PI Sunday — Personal Invitation Sunday

COMPLETE COMMITMENT SUNDAY

INVASION SUNDAY

Invade the community for Christ.

CAPACITY SUNDAY

TESTIMONY SUNDAY

I WILL CROWN HIM KING

Put Christ first on this Sunday.

PARK AND RIDE SUNDAY

Use this in connection with a new shuttle parking program of the church.

TEACH FAITHFULNESS

Some special days teach the importance of faithfulness in the Christian life:

LOYALTY SUNDAY

ROUND-UP SUNDAY

PRE-ROUND-UP SUNDAY

UNANIMOUS SUNDAY

SOMEDAY SUNDAY

SPRING ROUND-UP SUNDAY

ROLL CALL SUNDAY

DEDICATION SUNDAY

DIG OUT THE ENROLLMENT SUNDAY

OPEN DOORS

Certain days in Sunday School encourage church members to go to others and invite them to church. The title given to the day helps to open doors.

FRIEND DAY

NEIGHBOR SUNDAY

Invite your neighbor to attend.

PLUS ONE SUNDAY

Every day have one more present than the Sunday before.

DOUBLE-UP SUNDAY —OR — COME DOUBLE SUNDAY

Everyone is to bring someone else.

GRANDPARENTS AND GRANDCHILDREN SUNDAY

The grandchildren go to the grandparents and bring them to Sunday School.

BIRTHDAY SUNDAY

Invite friends to the party.

SEASONAL IDEAS

Some special days fit well with seasons of the year:

BACK TO SCHOOL SUNDAY

ANNIVERSARY SUNDAY

FATHER AND SON SUNDAY

MOTHER AND DAUGHTER SUNDAY

EARLY AMERICAN SUNDAY

FIRST SUNDAY

I LOVE AMERICA SUNDAY

This is a good way to celebrate the Sunday closest to July 4th.

EASTER SUNDAY

MOTHER'S DAY

FATHER'S DAY

FLAG DAY

RESOLUTION SUNDAY

EASTER PROMISE SUNDAY (APRIL)

BEAT THE HEAT SUNDAY

DEPENDENCE SUNDAY (JULY)

HARVEST SUNDAY (NOVEMBER)

SUMMER REVIVAL SUNDAY

THANKSGIVING DAY

INSTALLATION DAY

Install new teachers and officers.

OLD YEAR DAY

Use this on the last Sunday of the year.

NEW YEAR'S DAY

A DAY FOR REJOICING

This can be used on the Sunday after Christmas. The shepherds rejoiced after seeing Christ in the manger.

LET FREEDOM RING SUNDAY

HIS DAY

Use this title for Christmas Sunday.

PROMOTE MISSIONS

The Lord Jesus has commanded us to go into all the world and preach the Gospel. Some special days press the work of missions on the hearts of people:

UNION GOSPEL MISSION SUNDAY

INTERNATIONAL SUNDAY

Go after the people in your city from other nations.

BUS PASTORS' SUNDAY

MAGIC CARPET SUNDAY
(AROUND THE WORLD FOR CHRIST)

Invite all foreign-born citizens for Sunday School and church.

Give a nice memento (Testament, etc.) and flowers to the ladies (most foreigners like flowers more than we do).

WORLD'S SUNDAY SCHOOL DAY

Have people from foreign lands in Sunday School.

MISSIONARY DAY

WORLD CONQUEST (MISSIONARY SUNDAY)

A HEART FOR THE WORLD DAY

Place an emphasis on missions.

JEWISH SUNDAY

Have a saved Jew give his testimony and promote Jewish evangelism.

STIR THE MATTER OF SOUL WINNING

Some special days may be used to stir greater interest in soul winning:

CAMPAIGN FOR CHRIST

FRIEND SUNDAY

Everyone brings a friend.

LET'S GO FISHING

We are fishing for men.

JOHN 3 DAY

CHATTANOOGA SUNDAY

Seek to reach every area of the city for Christ. Have someone present from every area of the city.

OUTREACH SUNDAY

PERSONAL CONTACT SUNDAY

COMPEL SUNDAY

COMB THE COMMUNITY SUNDAY

LET YOUR LIGHT SHINE SUNDAY

STRANGERS' DAY

VISITING DAY

INVASION SUNDAY

MULTITUDE SUNDAY

SALVATION SUNDAY

NORTH OF THE RIVER WEEK

NORTH OF THE RIVER WEEK
Recognize people from certain areas of the city.

PROMOTE GREAT EVENTS

Special days are very helpful in promoting great events in the life of the church. They not only promote great events but also help to place necessary emphasis on upcoming meetings and activities.

RADIO ANNIVERSARY SUNDAY

PROMOTION SUNDAY

HOMECOMING SUNDAY

GET IN STEP SUNDAY
This is a great idea for the first Sunday of any campaign.

WELCOME HOME SUNDAY
Use this on the return of a pastor from a trip.

CENTURY SUNDAY

REVIVAL SUNDAY

GIANT STEP SUNDAY

GRAND FINALE SUNDAY
Use this on the final day of the campaign.

VICTORY SUNDAY

EMPHASIS SUNDAY

RALLY DAY

TOPPLE THE TOP SUNDAY
Seek to excel all that has been done in the past.

REVIVAL DAYS

"REVIVAL-5" DAYS
On the fifth Sunday of the month add five to all goals.

"BREAK THE RECORD SUNDAY"

TEN THOUSAND DAY
Set a number for your Sunday School goal, and title the day with that number.

PICTURE DAY

FINAL DAY MID-WINTER REVIVAL

PREMILLENNIAL SUNDAY
Teach the truth of the second coming of Christ.

FLY THE FLAG OF VICTORY SUNDAY
Use this for the closing day of a campaign.

FORWARD SUNDAY
Use this on the first Sunday of a Sunday School campaign.

RECOGNIZE AND REACH GROUPS
There are certain groups of people that need to be recognized and reached for Christ. Special days can help in this matter:

SENIOR SUNDAY
Recognize and present gifts to all seniors and graduates.

TEAM AND COACH DAY
Invite area high school teams and their coaches to be your special guest.

GUEST SUNDAY
Everyone should bring a guest.

OLD TIMERS' SUNDAY
Recognize all members who have belonged to the church for a certain time period.

NEWCOMERS' SUNDAY
Recognize all new members.

NEW CONVERT SUNDAY
Call attention to the zeal of new Christians.

LADIES' SUNDAY
Every lady is to bring a lady.

MEN'S DAY
Every man is to bring a man.

NEW FAMILIES' DAY
Recognize all the new families.

CHILDREN'S RALLY DAY

USHER SUNDAY

TEACHER-SUPERINTENDENT SUNDAY

TWIN SUNDAY

GRANDPARENTS' SUNDAY

BEYOND THE SUNSET SUNDAY

LEADERSHIP SUNDAY
Recognize all leaders.

LAW SUNDAY
Recognize and honor police and city officials.

TOURIST SUNDAY
Visit the motels.

VETERANS' DAY
Honor all branches of the military.

FAMILY DAY

ANNUAL SHUT-IN SUNDAY

T.A.G. SUNDAY
Have people present from the three state areas of Tennessee,
Alabama, and Georgia.

GEORGIA SUNDAY

YOUTH SUNDAY

CHILDREN'S DAY

HIGH SCHOOL SUNDAY

COLLEGE DAY

BABY DAY

"PARENT AND TEACHER" DAY
Seek to get all parents in Sunday School who are not already
attending.

"SENIOR CITIZENS" SUNDAY

TEACHER APPRECIATION DAY

SUNDAY SCHOOL WORKERS' APPRECIATION DAY

BACCALAUREATE SUNDAY

TRAILER FOLK SUNDAY

PUBLIC SERVANTS' SUNDAY
Invite all the public servants of the city
to be present.

CRADLE ROLL DAY
BEGINNERS' DAY
PRIMARY DEPARTMENT DAY
JUNIOR DEPARTMENT DAY
INTERMEDIATE DEPARTMENT DAY
OFFICERS' DAY
EDUCATION DAY
DAY SCHOOL DAY
HOME DAY
SERVICE MEN'S SUNDAY
GIDEONS' SUNDAY

Recognize the faithful ones of the church.

The Giant "Goliath." Costumed characters may be used at times for special emphasis.

28

If I Were A
Sunday School Teacher

"There is no painless way to follow Christ."   *Dr. Lee Roberson*

Every Sunday School teacher should seek the blessing of God upon his life and work. Do not be a "minimum teacher," doing just enough to get by or "hold your own." Serve Christ with certain goals and guidelines in mind. If I were a Sunday School teacher I would:

Know for Sure I Am Saved

To some this may seem repetitious: but the truth is, one can never do a work for God if he is troubled by doubts about his salvation. Know for sure you are saved. A lady came forward just outside of Atlanta on the last night of a revival meeting and said, "I have taught a Sunday School class in this church for fifteen years, and for the last three of those years I have known I am lost. Tonight I am coming to Christ."

Be Loyal to My Pastor

Every concerned Sunday School teacher loves and prays for his pastor. Let him know you are praying for him. God will not bless a teacher that has a complaining spirit toward his pastor. Follow the pastor's leadership.

Be Faithful to the Church

Our pastor has often said, "Everything rises or falls on leadership." A Sunday School teacher is a leader. If he is the right kind of leader, he will be faithful to every service of the church. It is impossible for a teacher to teach his class to be faithful if he is not faithful.

While one of our bus workers was visiting on her route, she met two little girls who were attending a Sunday School of another church. The girls said their Sunday School teacher came by for them each Sunday to take them to church. When asked by the bus worker, "Who is your pastor?" the girls replied, "We don't know him, our teacher brings us home after Sunday School; she never stays for church." That teacher needs to be relieved of her position. Faithfulness is a must.

Start Preparing My Lesson Early

The good Sunday School teacher realizes the value of preparation. It is not right for a teacher to stand before a class of pupils who need to hear the Word of God if that teacher is unprepared. Teachers who do not pay the price in preparation do not teach God's Word they simply get off on their own ideas and soon run out of anything to say. Prepare!

Teach the Bible

The greatest asset to any Sunday School is the uninterrupted study of the Word of God. Pupils in a Sunday School class need more than information about the Bible; they need to be fed the Word of God.

Be a Soul Winner

Every Sunday School teacher should seek to win souls. Set a goal to see someone saved each week from the class. If it is very young children being taught, seek to win at least one parent to Christ each week.

Have a Growing Class

There are multitudes of every age in every area who do not attend a Sunday School regularly. The prospects are plentiful. Any class will grow if the teacher works hard and uses basic principles of Sunday School growth.

Work on Enrollment

It is a proven fact that no less than 40 percent of a Sunday School class enrollment will be present on any given Sunday. We must seek to enroll anyone who is not already enrolled in a Sunday School class. Make these people more than prospects. Feel personally responsible for getting them under the sound of God's Word each week.

Pray for Each Class Member

Every Sunday School teacher should pray regularly for each member of his class. Let people know that you are praying for them. Make the roll book a prayer list. Also encourage each class member to pray for others in the class and to pray for the teacher.

Visit Every Absentee

The best time to visit someone who is absent from Sunday School is the first Sunday they miss. No matter who it is, everyone appreciates an expression of concern. Let people know they are important, they were missed, and they are needed.

Send a Class Letter

Contact with class members is vital to a Sunday School. One excellent way to stay in touch is by mail. Members can stay informed and also be prodded to attend faithfully. The letter can be mailed through bulk postage rate along with other class letters using the church's postal permit number.

Never Quit

It is interesting to see the zeal expressed in the work of a "new" Sunday School class. Later a class seems to reach a peak and, if not careful, fall into a slump. The most exciting work in the world is the work of Christ. Let us continue to go forward with determined enthusiasm, seeking the blessing of God upon our class with a never quit attitude.

29

Promote Scripture Memory

"There is no problem for which the Bible does not have an answer."

The Word of God is powerful. It is amazing how much of God's Word can be committed to memory by Sunday School pupils. Recently a young lady from our Sunday School memorized the entire book of II Timothy.

Make much of memorizing Bible verses in the Sunday School class. Present awards for verses memorized. There are many reasons for this emphasis.

THE LORD JESUS MEMORIZED SCRIPTURE

When Satan tempted the Lord Jesus in the wilderness, Christ defeated him with the Word of God, Matthew 4:4, 7, 10. Again and again our Lord said, "It is written," quoting from the book of Deuteronomy.

THE BIBLE KEEPS THE THOUGHT LIFE OF THE CHILD OF GOD CLEAN

"Wherewithal shall a young man cleanse his way? by taking heed thereto according to thy word. With my whole heart have I sought thee! O let me not wander from thy commandments. Thy word have I hid in mine heart, that I might not sin against thee." Psalm 119:9-11

SCRIPTURE MEMORY EQUIPS THE CHRISTIAN FOR SERVICE

"All scripture is given by inspiration of God, and is profitable for doctrine, for reproof, for correction, for instruction in righteousness: That the man of God may be perfect, throughly furnished unto all good works." II Timothy 3:16-17

Hints for Helping Memorize

Verses should be classified under a particular topic. When the verse is memorized, the reference should be repeated at the beginning and at the end of the verse. For many, the reference is more difficult to commit to memory than the verse.

Steps: Topic — Reference — Verse — Reference.

Repeat and Review

Someone has stated that repetition is the mother of learning. In Scripture memory, we must review the verse over and over again. Use the verse. It will soon be forgotten unless reviewed.

30

Set Goals

"Aimless wandering is the activity of defeated people."

Some are critical of goals, but they are necessary in the work of God. The business world makes use of goals. The political world uses goals. We need to see the value of goals in God's work. People need a purpose and direction in the Sunday School. Goals are a vital part of this.

Fix in Your Mind the Specific Goal You Desire

What do you want to see accomplished? One has to be more than a dreamer. What do we wish to see accomplished? If it is a class, what kind of goal do we have for the class as far as the number of people that we want to see reached and the training we want to give them? Fix in your mind the specific goal that you desire.

Determine to Pay the Price to Reach It

The difference between dreamers and goal-reachers is the willingness of the "reacher" to pay the price to do it. If we want to have a five hundred increase in Sunday School, that means we must start so many more new classes. That means we have to go out and enlist and train many more new people to work. Space must be provided. We have to go after people. Whatever the steps, there must be a willingness to pay the price to reach the goal. Now check yourself out. How high are your goals? What is firmly fixed in your mind to do with your life? What are you willing to pay?

Establish a Date to Reach It

The flesh is weak. We like to put things off and postpone, procrastinate. We must say, "By a certain time, this goal will become a reality." Set a date for it.

Develop a Plan for Attaining It

That does not mean at this point we have everything in its proper place as far as priorities are concerned; but it means we ought to take out a piece of paper or a notebook and write down everything we can think of that will have to be done to reach that goal: certain hours we will have to get up, things we will have to do, particular things we must read, and people we must enlist to be a part of the organization. Think of what will have to be done to reach the goal. This includes principles and people. Write them down! Put them in some sort of priority, and develop a plan for attaining the goal.

Start to Work Immediately

Do not sit around and say, "Well, where do I start? Which one do I do first?" Even if you do not have them in the exact order in which they ought to be, start at the top of the list and get something done. Be a man of action. There is too much talk and no walk today. A fellow called the other night and said, "You know, God wants me in children's work when I get out of school." I said, "Well, what about getting involved in the Afternoon Sunday School or the bus ministry?" He said, "Well, I do not really have time for anything now." He has as much time as anybody. He would not walk across the street to tell a lost child going to hell about Jesus. Oh, he would if you would twist his arm and tell him there was a boy standing over there weeping and crying and about to die lost. But we are saying, if you talk about something, then get busy and get at it. Be a person of action. Start to work immediately.

Keep the Goal Ever Before You

Remind yourself. Some say God has called them to the mission field; but if they are not careful, they will never go. Hear this, please. God has called some to preach, but they will never be in a church preaching the Word of God. God has called many to Christian education — to be a leader in a Christian educational institution — but they will never make it if they are not careful. If one does not keep his goal constantly before him, he will never reach it.

CHAPTER
31

Enroll More
In Sunday School

*"We are not in the percentage business;
we are in the people business."*

Although there is no set rule stating what method should be used in Sunday School enrollment, tradition controls many churches. It is more difficult to enroll in the average Sunday School than it is to join the church. Many teachers do not like to have their "average" lowered by so many on the roll who do not attend. Therefore, they decide to cut off the "dead wood" and show what a super group of saints attend their class. This "dead wood" cutting philosophy stems from pride and is the death of an evangelistic Sunday School class. When will we learn that the more we enroll, the more we have attending. Forget about the percentage that will not attend, and thank God for those that do attend. It would be much better to have 100 enrolled and have 50 in attendance than to have 60 enrolled and have 40 in attendance. A certain percent of the enrollment will attend. Perhaps never lower than 40 percent will attend. Therefore, the way to increase attendance is to increase enrollment. The more we have attending our Sunday Schools, the more we will see saved; and the best way to increase attendance is to increase enrollment — so ENROLL, ENROLL, ENROLL.

Most visitors in a typical Sunday School class are expected to visit three times before they can be enrolled. Although this is practiced by most, no one is willing to admit that it is church policy. Whether practiced or adopted as church policy, it is the wrong way to enroll new people in Sunday School.

Any person — anywhere, any time — that is not already enrolled in a Sunday School should be on the Sunday School roll of a Bible teaching Sunday School class. When that particular person is enrolled, he becomes someone's responsibility.

Cards, letters, phone calls, personal visits, and other methods should be used to encourage the faithful attendance of this new member. There are one million more lost people in this world every week. God help us to get them under the sound of His Word. Many cults have made use of the interest of people in Bible study. It is time we who truly believe the Word of God get busy and enroll the unsaved and unenlisted multitudes in Sunday School.

THINK WHAT COULD BE DONE

If one person enrolled two new Sunday School members each week for one year, he would increase the Sunday School enrollment by 100.

Look what some could do:

4 per week for 1 year —	200
6	300
8	400
10	500
12	600
14	700
16	800
18	900
20	1,000

If 10 Sunday School teachers in a local church enrolled one new member each week for one year, they could increase the Sunday School enrollment by 500.

The old tried and proven methods of Sunday School growth are:

Locate the prospects   Enlist and train leaders
Enlarge the organization   Go after the people
Provide space

These methods work. We need to put each of these steps to practice.

One pastor recently stated that he determined to see a new class of adults in his church. He found a vacant room in his building and worked all day Saturday enrolling members in his "new class." When the day's work came to a close, he had enrolled 34 members; and on Sunday morning he had 15 of these brand new adults in his class. It can be done!

Work on increasing enrollment; and never drop anyone from the roll unless that person has died, moved out of the city, or joined another church.

32

Stay with the Word of God

> *"The greatest asset to any Sunday School is the uninterrupted teaching of the Word of God."*

The greatest asset to any Sunday School is the Word of God. We are not engaged in the task of giving people the opinions of this present day but rather in teaching them the eternal Word of God. Make much of the Bible. Insist on the uninterrupted teaching of God's Word each week in each class. The Bible is the Book of books.

GIVE THE BIBLE ITS PROPER PLACE

The Bible should be used by every leader of the Sunday School. It must be given its rightful place, and nothing should be allowed to substitute for God's Word in the Sunday School class.

The Bible and the Sunday School Teacher

What a glorious opportunity the Sunday School teacher has in giving his pupils God's Word. Teach it to them. Teach to love, honor, depend on, and respect the Bible. The Bible will change their lives. It is a living book. In Isaiah 55:10-11, God says, "For as the rain cometh down, and the snow from heaven, and returneth not thither, but watereth the earth, and maketh it bring forth and bud, that it may give seed to the sower, and bread to the eater: So shall my word be that goeth forth out of my mouth: it shall not return unto me void, but it shall accomplish that which I please, and it shall prosper in the thing whereto I sent it."

These verses alone should challenge the teacher to study God's Word and prepare. He can go before his class each week with confidence and courage, knowing that the Bible, when given out to people, will accomplish what the Lord wants to see come to pass in the lives of people.

The Bible and the Sunday School Pupil

The Bible is the Sunday School textbook. It is the only textbook used in the Sunday School. All the aims and purposes of the class should come from the Bible. Good helps and visual aids are valuable, but they should never be allowed to substitute for the Bible. Every pupil should have the Bible in hand as he enters the class and should use it during Sunday School.

The Bible and the Lost

A growing Sunday School class will have lost people visiting in it each week. God's Word will speak to their hearts. The Bible says, "For the Word of God is quick, and powerful, and sharper than any two-edged sword, piercing even to the dividing asunder of soul and spirit, and of the joints and marrow, and is a discerner of the thoughts and intents of the heart." Hebrews 4:12.

The Bible and the Saved

It is impossible to build strong Christians without the Word of God. The Bible is the Christian's food. There is no such thing as a victorious Christian apart from the Word of God. The study of the Bible will not only strengthen the Christian but will also safeguard him against sin. It is his weapon of defense; "Thy word have I hid in mine heart, that I might not sin against thee." Psalms 119:11. It is also his weapon of offense; ". . .the sword of the Spirit, which is the Word of God." Ephesians 6:17. The Christian should be given God's Word in Sunday School and he should receive principles on how he can study the Bible for himself.

WORK ON HAVING A "BIBLE-BRINGING SUNDAY SCHOOL"

Award people for having their Bible and attaining Bible knowledge. Recognize those who read regularly the Word of God. It is impossible to overemphasize the prominent place of the eternal Word of God in the Sunday School.

33

Make the Most of the Sunday School Lesson

"The Lord does not bless us for what we are in public, but rather for what we are in the secret places of our lives."

Catch the Attention
Through the Opening of the Lesson

The opening should be brief and should focus attention on the lesson. That which appeals to ear or eye will captivate interest from the beginning, as:

1. A question, "What would YOU do if. . .?"

2. Some action — displaying an object, a map, a picture.

3. A story or illustration.

Hold the Interest
Throughout the Main Body of the Lesson

Proceed from the KNOWN to the UNKNOWN. Review briefly the preceding lesson, tying it to the lesson for today. A word or two may also tie the lesson up with the lesson for next week. Use illustrations about familiar things they already know. (As we get acquainted with our pupils and what they already know, our teaching will improve).

Continually refer to the Bible. "Let's see what God's Word has to say about it." Keep it plain WHO is speaking, TO WHOM He is speaking, and FOR WHAT PURPOSE He is speaking. Even with small children we can teach them to think of God's Word as the source of our standards. With older children, verses can be looked up and explained by them.

Make use of maps and blackboards as the lesson proceeds (unless flannelgraph is used).

Stimulate the pupil's participation. For smaller children: Workbooks, if possible, re-telling of story, expression through simple drawings or coloring books; through dramatization. For older children: Encourage them to ask questions, "What happened? Where? When? Why?" Use workbooks, re-telling, dramatization, projects.

Create a Desire to Live According to God's Will

The teacher must now apply the lesson to the pupil — he must show that God's Word is related to the pupil's life. This can be done in such a way as to create a desire for spiritual things. The APPLICATION should be brief and to the point, but it should be PERSONAL.

Inspire Action in the Closing Part of the Lesson

Each Bible lesson, well taught, ought to be a challenge to some type of action. It should result in some small step closer to God in faith and obedience. To some of the pupils, it may be to trust Christ and to receive Him as Saviour. To others, it might be a challenge to bow to His authority as Lord. To older ones, it might be to a deeper prayer life, to more Bible study, to witnessing for Him. To some, the desired action — to serve others for Jesus' sake.

34

Use Effective Discipline

*"Individuals are important to God. We
must never lose our personal touch."*

The tremendous discipline problems encountered today in a
growing work for God cannot be compared to simple problems
of the past. This writer has personally witnessed children steal-
ing, breaking into offices, ripping seats, beating and pushing
smaller children, threatening bodily harm to teachers, using
abusive language; gangs actually attacking teachers; and a
host of other problems taking place. Some would say, "It is just
too much to take. Let us just call off our efforts to reach them."
The result of this attitude is finalized in multitudes going to
hell when they could have been reached. We must never give
up! Realize the value of precious souls and the ability of God to
change lives.

WHY DO THEY MISBEHAVE?

In order to use correct discipline we must understand the
root of the problem. It is not enough just to treat the
symptoms.

1. **Human Beings Are Sinners By Nature.** The Word of God is
   clear in stating we are born in sin. We are sinners by conception,
   by choice, and by conduct.
2. **Satan Is Against the Work of God.** Any way you look at it, if we
   are doing a work for God, Satan will fight it. He has won the victory
   when we develop a defeated attitude and give up.
3. **Bad Home Situations.** It is impossible to adequately describe the
   pitiful condition of most homes in America. At our church we insist
   that a teacher visit the homes of his pupils. This enables him to
   understand more fully the problems he faces.
4. **Overcrowded Rooms.** In an aggressive growing Sunday School
   the problem of overcrowded classrooms must always be dealt with.
   This overcrowding creates discipline problems. We are faced many

times with poor seating, noise distractions, and other room problems.

5. **Physical Disabilities.** One teacher was guilty of correcting a child for talking out too loud in the class. Later she discovered the child was deaf and did not realize the loudness of his voice. Many poor children come to Sunday School fatigued. They have had very little rest because of fighting in the home during the night. Many have poor vision, retardation, hearing problems, and sickness.

6. **No Instruction on Proper Behavior.** We must realize that many who come to our churches have never been instructed in proper behavior and must be taught even the simplest rules of courtesy.

7. **Permissive Public Schools.** In many public schools today the authority is in the students' hands. The teachers and administrators work in fear. The students are actually in control, if those public school officials would ever admit it. When pupils come to the Sunday School with this kind of attitude, problems will soon develop.

8. **Fear.** Many children are afraid. They enter a new room and meet new people. They do not know how they will be treated. They react out of fear.

9. **They Are Starving for Love and Attention.** Many children in America today know nothing of what it means to be loved and cared for. The only way they know to get attention is to misbehave.

HELPS IN DISCIPLINE

As long as we obey Christ in going after souls, we shall be faced with discipline problems from those we bring to our churches. We cannot let up on our evangelistic outreach; therefore, we must employ the best methods of discipline. The aggressive bus ministry and the obedience of the Great Commission to go to all people, which includes the slums, housing projects, and inner-city areas, has brought to our churches multitudes of "problem people." God help us — we must help them!

1. *The Bible Is Our Guidebook*

The Word of God is the answer to all life's problems. We find direction for discipline within its pages. Proverbs 3:12 states, "For whom the Lord loveth he correcteth; even as a father the son in whom he delighteth." The Bible teaches that there must be a relationship of authority — God and His children, a father and his son, the teacher and his pupil. Someone must be in charge and the other under submission. It also teaches that the discipline must be founded on love for the one corrected. You discipline and correct one because you love him. It states further that the one doing the disciplining must delight in the one he has to discipline: the teacher must have the attitude of joy and thankfulness at the opportunity to have his pupils.

2. *Nothing Is Impossible with God*

All things are possible. God can enable a teacher to handle his problems, and at the same time He can work in the life of that one who needs to be disciplined.

3. *Seek Direction from the Lord*

We are involved in a spiritual work. We need the Holy Spirit's direction in knowing how to act.

4. *Pray Much*

Pray for yourself. Pray for all those who help you. Pray for each pupil in the class and also pray much for those who have been causing problems.

5. *Realize the Value of Those You Teach*

Think what God can make out of people. See more than what sits before you each week. Get a vision of what God can do with those precious lives. Do not make the mistake of equating their unruly behavior with their personal worth. Learn the name of each pupil, and delight in the opportunity you have to teach them.

6. *Discipline Only When Necessary*

Punishment is necessary for a direct challenge to authority, not because we are inconvenienced. Many are quick to condemn a parent who punishes a child for accidentally breaking a glass, when in reality the teacher is just as guilty for punishing a pupil for going beyond a boundary of which he was not even aware. There is a difference between misunderstanding a request and willfully rebelling against authority.

7. *Preparation Is a Must*

Prepare your own heart and mind for the task before you. Be thankful for each pupil. Be very familiar with the material you plan to teach. Be sure that the room is exactly the way you wish for it to be.

8. *Act Calmly – Do Not Let Self Get out of Control*

Sometimes the best step toward correcting a pupil who is out of control is to be very much under control yourself. Usually, lashing back with aggression only makes the situation worse.

9. *Use Positive Correction*

Let each pupil know that you have made preparation for the day and you are very disappointed at misbehavior problems. Make statements like, "I know you can do better," "I know you are capable," "Seek to please the Lord Jesus with your behavior."

10. *Teach the Pupil How*
To Express Himself in an Acceptable Manner

Everyone has a desire to be accepted and to receive the approval of someone. One big problem we are faced with today is that children know so very little about respect, common courtesy, and good manners. We must take the time to teach them how to express themselves in an acceptable manner.

11. *Isolate Problem Cases*

Find the culprit in the room who is causing the problem. Be very careful about trying to correct a real rebel in the presence of the rest of the class. You may win in the end, but many ugly things may be said and done by the "problem causer" before you are finished. Sometimes just the simple act of separating the person responsible for starting the problem will solve the difficulty. You may be able to put this person "one-on-one" with a worker that can spend the necessary time with this particular person.

12. *What Christ Can Make*

Whatever the problems encountered, we must determine to go after all people with the saving message of the Lord Jesus. He can make a new creature out of a lost, rebellious sinner.

35

Helpful Hints to Use in Getting People to Attend

"The greatest strain upon the servant of God is the pull of the people."

Many Christian workers have gotten terribly disappointed over the broken promises and commitments of those whom they have contacted. Why don't people come to our Sunday School?

The person visited has expressed an interest in Bible study and has agreed to come to Sunday School; but between this time and his actual attendance, some of these questions will arise:

What will the Bible study be like?

Who will be in my class?

Where is the church located?

How do I get to the church from here?

When I arrive, how will I know where to go?

If I do not have transportation, will someone pick me up?

Is there someone I can contact if I have a question?

Very few people decide to do something new without investigating it, having second thoughts, and asking many questions.

How Can the Church Provide the Right Answers to These Questions?

1. Work on making a good first impression at the time of enrollment.
2. Leave good printed material about the church. (This must include where to go and what to do when he attends the first time.)
3. Describe the type of Bible study, and tell him of others who will be there.

4. Leave the name and address of someone he can contact for further information.

5. Be sure to check on the matter of transportation.

The materials left in the home will keep reminding the person of the importance of Bible study and what to expect at your church.

Once a person arrives for the first Bible study, he begins to examine the situation to see if it is what he expected it to be. He will think of such things as:

- Do I fit in this group? Will I be accepted?
- What will I be expected to do? Will I be called on for anything?
- Who is in charge? Will I like this person? Will he like me?
- What other activities do these people have as a group other than Bible study?

The Church Can Help with These Questions in the Following Ways

1. Be very prayerful about who is in charge of the class. He needs to be a strong leader. He must be a very good Bible teacher and show compassion for others.

2. The meeting place must be attractive and relatively easy to find.

3. The new person should not, as a rule, be called upon to do or say much in the first session.

4. Plan to make the new member welcome, and be sure there is a sense of readiness in the class.

5. Mention can be made of other activities the class engages in (mission projects, socials, etc.).

6. Assign someone to contact this new member personally in the days ahead. We are seeking to get the message of salvation to people, see them saved, baptized, and actively involved in the local church.

If we work to relieve the fears of these new people and endeavor to make them feel important, we have made great strides toward helping them in their relationship to Christ. Make much of the Word of God. There is a hunger in the hearts of people to know what the Bible really has to say.

One last thought — always be specific when inviting someone to church or Sunday School. Ask the person to be present *this* Sunday. Tell him the exact time you plan to be by for him. Get a commitment. It is of absolutely no value to extend vague, general invitations.

Faithful nursery workers make a tremendous difference.

36

Teacher –
Take a Check-Up

"The best ability is dependability."
Dr. Bob Jones, Sr.

	YES	NO
Preparation		
Do I plan my work far enough ahead?	—	—
Do I spend enough time upon each lesson?	—	—
Do I set a goal for each quarter?	—	—
Can I state, in a simple sentence, my goals in each lesson?	—	—
Do I make suggestions for pupil's preparation for next week?	—	—
Does every member of the class have the necessary materials?	—	—
Teaching Methods		
Do I strive for variety?	—	—
Do I open the lesson with prayer?	—	—
Are my opening statements challenging, interesting, and clear?	—	—
Do I stick to the lesson?	—	—
Do I apply it to life?	—	—
Do I summarize to tie together all the loose ends?	—	—
Do I link my thoughts together to make a complete picture?	—	—
Do I do all the talking?	—	—
Do I argue?	—	—
Do I listen to the opinions of others?	—	—

Am I attempting to do the teaching
rather than presenting the
teachings of Jesus Christ and the Bible?   ___   ___

The Class

Is my class made up
as nearly as possible of people
of the same age and interests?   ___   ___
Is my classroom
attractive and comfortable?   ___   ___
Is my class too large? Too small?   ___   ___

The Teacher

Do I start and close the period on time?   ___   ___
Do I use all the time to advantage,
or do I waste time?   ___   ___
Am I friendly?   ___   ___
Do I make my class feel at home?   ___   ___
Do I get my students
acquainted with each other?   ___   ___
Am I personally concerned for the
spiritual welfare of each pupil?   ___   ___
Do I pray for them?   ___   ___
Do I encourage them
to come to church?   ___   ___
Do I help them
outside the class period?   ___   ___
Do I keep check
on their spiritual welfare?   ___   ___

37

Attendance Boosters in Your Children's Classes

"W.O.R.K. is still the best formula for success."

The following ideas may be used to add variety and interest to Sunday School classes. These are especially appropriate to children's classes.

Happy Day Contest

Why not try a Happy Day Contest that could also be an attendance booster. See how many days during the month you have new children attend. Each time a new child attends, put up another happy face. Pin the happy faces in a conspicuous place where the children of the class can see the progress. Of course, if no new children attend then the sad face is displayed.

Let's Lick Absenteeism

Place a large lollipop sucker on a board with each pupil's name under the sucker. At the end of one month each person receives his sucker if he has been present each Sunday of the month — lick absenteeism!

Valentine Idea

Make a big heart out of posterboard. Cut the heart into enough pieces so that each class member will have a piece of the heart. The Sunday before Valentine's, send a piece of the heart home with each child, with instructions to bring it back with him next week to make the heart complete. A separate heart can be made for visitors, and each pupil can take a section of that heart to give to a friend to return also.

King and Queen Contest

This idea will add lots of excitement to any Sunday School

contest. Purchase two crowns — one for a king and the other for a queen. Announce all during the campaign that a king and queen will be crowned. The girl and boy who do the most outstanding job will be king and queen.

Use a Lollipop Tree

Make a lollipop tree from a piece of styrofoam (in the shape of a cone). Purchase Tootsie-Roll pops and stick them in the tree. This idea can be used for new children brought to class or for memory verses learned. If a child brings a new child, he can come and pick a lollipop from the tree. Also, you can unwrap a few lollipops and put in a small piece of paper which says, "Surprise." Then wrap it up again and put it on the tree. If a child picks this lollipop, he can also choose a gift from the surprise box. The surprise box contains inexpensive gift items.

What's the Temperature of Your Heart?
Four-Week Contest

Make a picture of a thermometer for each child. Divide the thermometer by degrees from zero to 98.6 degrees. The thermometer will rise toward normal each week. The normal thing for every boy and girl to do is attend Sunday School and memorize the Bible.

> Rules:
> Attendance — add 10 degrees
> Memory Verse Learned — add 10 degrees
> Visitor Brought This Month — add 18.6 degrees

Comb Idea

This is just an added idea to promote faithful attendance. The teacher purchases a comb for each of the pupils and writes the name of the child on the comb. They are told that they can have the comb at the end of the quarter; but each Sunday morning, if they miss the class, one tooth of the comb will be broken out. You will be surprised at the number of parents who have to delay a trip out of town because little Sue doesn't want her comb spoiled.

Christmas Attendance Idea

Purchase a small mesh Christmas stocking for each child, and hang it up on a board. As each one comes to class each

Sunday of December before Christmas, place a small wrapped gift in the stocking. On the Sunday before Christmas, present each child with his stocking. The gifts can be inexpensive, and the child will try to be out to get a small gift each time.

Grab Bag

Place in a large paper bag many small items such as sticks of gum, lollipops, bookmarks, picture text cards, etc. — any odds and ends will do. Fasten to the end of each of these a string, the other end of which protrudes out of the top of the bag. Each child who has been present and on time for five consecutive weeks at class is given an opportunity to pull a string and draw an article from the grab bag, sight unseen.

38

Win Every Member Of the Class to Christ

"The crowning work of a Christian is winning and witnessing to others."
Dr. Lee Roberson

The Sunday School is more than getting people to church. It is more than Bible teaching; it is soul winning. We must seek the salvation of all those on our class rolls. The great Evangelist D. L. Moody had his heart stirred to win the lost by a compassionate Sunday School teacher. This is the story as told by D. L. Moody.

For a long time after my conversion I didn't accomplish anything. It was in 1860 the change came. In the Sunday School I had an able, delicate young man as one of the teachers. I knew his burning piety and assigned him to a class of girls, the worst of the school. They were outbreaking, but he got along with them better than anyone else had done. One day he was absent and I tried to teach them, but failed. The next morning he came into the store tottering and bloodless, and threw himself on some boxes. I asked, "What is the matter?" He said, "I've been bleeding at the lungs and the doctors have given me up to die." "You are not afraid to die." "No," he answered, "but I am afraid to stand before God and tell Him I left all those girls unsaved! Oh, if I could only see them saved!"

I got a carriage and drove that dying man to each one of their homes, and to each girl, in faint voice, he (the teacher) said, "I must leave you! I am going to die, but I want you to come to the Saviour!" And then he prayed as I have never heard a man pray before. For ten days he labored and prayed. At the end of that time the last girl had yielded to the Saviour. The night before he left for the South, they met at his house. All were saved, and it was the gate of Heaven. He prayed, I prayed, and each of them prayed and we sang, "Blest Be the Tie That Binds." Next morning, without any concerted arrangements, every girl came to the depot to say good-bye. It was a second gate of Heaven, though in one respect so sad. The gong sounded. He was supported on to the platform, and he sang,

> Shall we meet beyond the river
> Where the surges cease to roll,
> Where in all that bright forever
> Sorrow ne'er shall press the soul?

And as the train moved off they responded,

> We shall meet in that blessed harbor,
> When our stormy voyage is o'er.
> We shall meet and cast the anchor
> By that fair celestial shore!

Those ten tiring days of toil to reach a class of lost young ladies transformed D. L. Moody. He, who long yearned to be a millionaire merchant and to build the biggest Sunday School in Chicago, saw in those ten days the whitened fields of harvest, the brevity and frailty of life, the immensity and importance of eternity's values. There and then D. L. Moody sold out to Christ to win all the souls he could while it was harvest hour.

CHAPTER

39

Invest Your Life In the Work of Christ

"We have just one life to live. If we invest it wrongly, we have all eternity to regret it."

The story of Edward Kimball tells how one life invested for Christ as a Sunday School teacher bears abundant fruit.

Mr. Edward Kimball, a Sunday School teacher bears abundant fruit.

Mr. Edward Kimball, a Sunday School teacher in Boston, loved boys and sought them for Jesus. Through him a boy named D. L. Moody came to Jesus in 1858.

D. L. Moody, while preaching in England in 1879, had a great spiritual influence on F. B. Meyer.

F. B. Meyer won a young college student, J. W. Chapman to Christ.

J. W. Chapman brought the message of Christ to a baseball player named Billy Sunday. The Lord used him in a powerful way in evangelism and the temperance movement.

These names are all known in the Lord's Hall of Fame. It all began with Mr. Kimball. God needs more teachers to love boys and girls, and men and women. Mr. Kimball tells in his own words how D. L. Moody came to know Christ as his Saviour:

"I determined to speak to him about Christ and about his soul, and started down to Holton's shoe store. When I was nearly there I began to wonder whether I ought to go in just then during business hours. I thought that possibly my call might embarrass the boy, and that when I went away the other clerks would ask who I was, and taunt him with my efforts in trying to make him a good boy. In the meantime I had passed

149

the store, and discovering this I determined to make a dash for it and have it over.

I found Moody in the back part of the building wrapping up shoes. I went up to him at once, and putting my hand on his shoulder I made what I afterwards felt was a very weak plea for Christ. I don't know just what words I used, nor could Mr. Moody tell. I simply told him of Christ's love for him and the love Christ wanted in return. That was all there was. It seemed the young man was just ready for the light that then broke upon him, and there, in the back of that store in Boston, he gave himself and his life to Christ."

40

Have a Never-Quit Attitude

> *"The test of your Christian character and desire to serve God is not in what it takes to get you started, but rather in what it takes to stop you after you start."*

A certain person in 1831 failed in business. In 1832, he was defeated for the legislature. In 1833, he again failed in business. In 1834, he was elected to the legislature. In 1835, his sweetheart died. In 1836, he had a nervous breakdown. In 1838, he was defeated for the legislative speaker's place. In 1840, he was defeated for elector. In 1843, he was defeated for Congress. In 1855, he was defeated for Senate. In 1856, he was defeated for vice-president. In 1858, he was defeated for Senate. But in 1860, the record changed. He was elected President. Although he had many defeats, Abraham Lincoln considered them only temporary and turned them into stepping stones to success because he had a never-quit attitude. How did he get it?

HAVE A DEFINITE PURPOSE BACKED BY A BURNING DESIRE TO FULFILL IT

Here again is the word "purpose." Do not desire to be "just a teacher," or leader, or to have "just any place" in Christian service. Aspire for great things for the glory of God. Have a definite purpose backed by a burning desire to fulfill it!

HAVE A DEFINITE PLAN
EXPRESSED IN CONTINUOUS ACTION

State, "This is my desire." Here is the plan, and this plan is going to be carried out. Be busy at it, day after day, week after week, until the desire becomes a reality. People who quit are people who think there is nothing to do. Think about that. They are people who have no vision or dream. They do not aspire for anything or do anything. They just get to the place where every day is just another hum-ho day — just another day, with no purpose, no burning desire. They are backed by nothing and driven by nothing. They are not trying to achieve anything.

CLOSE YOUR MIND TO ALL NEGATIVE INFLUENCES

Now this is a dangerous statement. Be flexible, roll with the punches, seek self-improvement; but when you know you are right — do not let the devil or any other demon-possessed thing on the face of God's earth keep you from seeing your dream come to pass. Determine that nothing, absolutely nothing, will sidetrack you. Close your mind to all negative influences. Close your mind even if it is to your relatives and friends. Close your mind to all negative influences. The test of your Christian character and your desire to serve God is not what it takes to get you started; but rather, what it takes to stop you after you start for God. Many a person has run to an altar and made a vow to a leader to do a certain thing. That was easy. But staying at it until the task has been completed is the test of your character.

KEEP YOUR EYES ON THE LORD JESUS CHRIST

Life is filled with many storms and trials. We must keep our eyes on the Saviour to live victoriously. Friends will fail, businesses and cherished plans will fail; but Christ cannot fail. Many sidetracked saints need to take their eyes off people and "things" and get them back on the Lord Jesus Christ.